T0193029

REVELATIONS

THE TRUE STORY OF REV. DR. JOSEPH LEO
THERIAULT

HARRY S. WYLIE

Published by:
Trine Day LLC
PO Box 577
Walterville, OR 97489
1-800-556-2012
www.TrineDay.com
trineday@icloud.com

Library of Congress Control Number: 2021905632

Wylie, Harry S.
Revelations: The True Story of Rev. Dr. Joseph Leo Theriault—1st ed.
p. cm.

Epub (ISBN-13) 978-1-63424-353-7
Mobi (ISBN-13) 978-1-63424-354-4
Print (ISBN-13) 978-1-63424-352-0
1. Theriault, Joseph Leo. -- 1934-2020 2. Catholic Church -- Clergy -- Sexual be-
havior. 3. Child sexual abuse -- Catholic Church. 4. Child sexual abuse by clergy
-- Canada. 5. Psychiatry and religion. I. Wylie,, Harry S. II. Title

FIRST EDITION
10 9 8 7 6 5 4 3 2

Distribution to the Trade by:
Independent Publishers Group (IPG)
814 North Franklin Street
Chicago, Illinois 60610
312.337.0747
www.ipgbook.com

He Killed My Sister

Kill, maime, dismember, destroy
I'll play with your life like a childs toy.
A burning hatred down deep inside,
That only your blood could ever satisfy.
The torture of your death I soon begin
Not knowing remorse not feeling for sin
I will bite and tear into the flesh of your neck.
Start to giggle as I witness your body a wreck

–Juvenile Patient

TABLE OF CONTENTS

Chapter I

PARADOX

In my early days as a priest my life seemed to be endemic with ambiguity; sin, sexuality, contraception, and the confessional being but four incongruities.

As a young priest my notion of salvation was mathematically oriented in the sense that when one dies God will calculate all the virtuous activity against all the sins one has committed. If good deeds outweighed your sins, you were saved; if not tough luck. However, the Gospel is of the love of God and not of bookkeeping. It brings to mind the story of the Prodigal Son, also known as the Parable of the Lost Son, where Jesus demonstrated what it means to be lost, how heaven celebrates with joy when the lost are found, and how the loving Father longs to save people. In the parable the lost son was accepted back by his father with unconditional love. Checks and balances were not considered. What a powerful message. No bookkeeping, just our loving God. This should be the Christian way.

Another concern I had when I started my ministry was the problem of contraception; it was forbidden by the Vatican as being a sin against the Law of the Church. Sexual intercourse is for the survival of the species and anything blocking natural law is a sin; ergo, contraception is evil. This approach was influenced by the dualistic belief a person is composed of two parts: the soul created by God and the body coming from the devil. Each mortal is in a tug-of-war between God and the devil. Starting with the premise the body is from the devil, any sexual pleasure is therefore a sin. This obviously opened a wide door for preachers who like to send everyone to hell. God only knows how many preachers used sexuality to instill the fear and call it fear of God among their parishioners. This can be used as a two bladed sword by such priests, "If I can't enjoy sex, then neither will you."

Human sexuality should be considered or dealt with the same way as other human emotions and drives. We share many drives with other animal classifications but being an advanced and developed species we have to learn to control these sensations. Hunger is a drive that assures the survival of the individual. When hungry the strongest animal will satiate himself without caring if there will be food left for the weakest. Animals don't have table manners; they eat to survive. They can eat alone as they don't need company. Humans on the other hand have developed a social aspect to eating. Children learn to dine with others, have good table manners and share. We celebrate special events by drinking and eating together. At the Last Supper Jesus said, "Do this in remembrance of me" (Luke 22:19). The Grand Seminary was an enormous departure from the Last Supper as we ate most meals in silence.

We also share sexual drive with lower animals. Having sex and making love are two different things. One is very selfish and the other is an expression of love between two people. Unlike the lower faunae, human sexual activity goes beyond solely reproduction. It is a very strong expression of love between two people comparable to the love of God for his people. Or at least should be. Unfortunately, this is rarely the case.

When I was about ten years old, I remember hearing a priest in the pulpit saying, "Ladies if you are doing the dishes and your husband asks for sex, you must leave the dishes then and there and do your duty as a wife." It was the man's right and the woman's duty. There was more than one occasion when the wife told me their husbands asked for sex before going to hospital to have a baby.

Young girls were brainwashed about sex. Parents felt if their daughters were scared enough, they would be virgins on their wedding day and could truthfully wear white. Mothers felt it was their duty to protect their daughter's virginity – but at what cost? Young girls were conditioned that premarital sex was a sin but not so after her wedding day; it was if a switch was flipped after the "I dos" were promised at the altar. It is little wonder many women went through married life without ever experiencing an orgasm. Woe be the woman who gave birth under nine months and wore white at her wedding. Yentas were omnipresent.

Advent and Lent was a time of penance therefore Catholics could not marry during this time without the bishop's permission and he would only give thus if the woman was pregnant; a "shotgun marriage." God help the young man who perpetrated the malicious deed and tried to skip his marital obligation.

The bedroom also created major problems for some young couples who wanted to follow the Law of the Church. If the young woman enjoyed sexual activity the rhythm method was very restraining. It was an ethical confusion often brought to the priest for moral advice. The priest was caught between a rock and a hard place; the teaching of the church and the young couple's dilemma. The priest generally tried to neutralize the challenge without making it worse. A young priest struggling with his own celibacy, not truly understanding the circumstances, had to be Solomonic – wise, reasonable and discretional under trying circumstances – with a millennium old enigma. It was the blind leading the blind. Often, I heard the complaint, "My wife is so fertile I hardly touch her and she's pregnant. The rhythm method doesn't work, and we can't afford another kid. What can we do?"

One priest I knew in my childhood had more compassion than the Church. He surreptitiously distributed condoms to those who could ill-afford any additions to their family knowing full well the Church considered this a mortal sin.

The teaching of the church is clear, no contraceptive or you commit a sin. The choice is between abstinence and sin. Many priests, perhaps hopefully most, take the pastoral approach, the Good Shepherd approach, whereby the shepherd takes care of his sheep individually. Writing about contraception as a sin in the 21st century seems like a fairy tale but in the past it was a reality of the day.

Between the two Great Wars having a large family was strongly promoted. It assured the survival of the ethnic groups, or clans or nations. French Canada was no different. The Old Testament incessantly promotes large families; ergo, large families were considered a blessing. Farmers needed many sons to run the farm prior to John Deere and the tractor.

Sterility was a malediction.

Contraception was always a problem in the Catholic Church while it was a non-issue with Protestants. When it was a mixed marriage it became a major conundrum. A Catholic wife didn't want more children, but her faith prevented her from using contraceptive devices. Her Protestant husband desired for her to have her tubes tied while donning a macho mien and refusing a vasectomy.

In the 1970s and 1980s the Vatican was still damning contraception while married couples and their priests were taking a more pragmatic approach. The cogent cleric interpreted the law of the Church as an ideal objective of perfection while understanding they were dealing with non-perfect humans. A couple trying to live an ideal life but agonized on failure always had the confessional for absolution; the pastoral way of dealing with an enigma.

An enormous responsibility for the priest is the confessional. With this responsibility, however, comes influence and power. The priest in the confessional is like a judge of the Supreme Court. He listens, makes judgment and decides exculpation or condemnation; should he forgive the sins or not. Forgiveness is accompanied by a penance based on Jesus telling his disciples in John 20:23 "Receive the Holy Spirit. If you forgive anyone his sins, they are forgiven; if you withhold forgiveness from anyone, it is withheld."

For priests who are control freaks the confessional gives them an excellent opportunity to abuse their power. They can refuse absolution and then refuse Holy Communion. It can be very humiliating and very traumatic for a parishioner because "out of the church there is no salvation" and no salvation means one is going to hell. Add the "Secret of Confession" to an abusive or controlling priest and you have a child in a candy store.

The confessional could also be used as a conduit to assignations or prey. If a female penitent revealed her promiscuity, she could become prey for a sexually aroused priest. If a young boy confessed his dilemma over his masculinity, he could become "fair game."

After my ordination I was a very happy man. I was away from the monastic existence and reached my life's goal of being a priest. The emotion I felt after ordination and my first mass was wonderful. I loved celebrating mass and preaching and being asked for blessing was most gratifying. I loved helping my parishioners, but I was uncomfortable with the confessional.

When I was ordained most Catholics went to confession at least once a month and many once a week. Priests were available for acknowledgment half an hour before mass and many parishioners felt they could not receive Holy Communion unless they first received absolution. There was a rush on confessionals at Christmas, Easter and the first Friday of the month. The first Friday of the month was a very popular devotion day dedicated to the Sacred Heart of Jesus; referring to a loving God rather than a judgmental God. It was erroneously rumored, and widely believed, if you received the Holy Communion on nine consecutive first Fridays you were assured salvation; a recipe to get to Heaven. It was like finding the fountain of youth.

Before my conferment I had always gone to confession and learned its ritual but after ordination I was uncomfortable with the charge and disconcerted about forgiving sins. I was not God. Moreover, the absolution was said in Latin and I felt it wrong forgiving sins in a language no one understood. It took a lot of faith. Going to confession and communion

4

is acceptable but it should not distract from the fundamental commandment of love thy neighbor as you love thyself.

Vatican II changed so much, including the confessional. Confession went from Judgment to the Sacrament of Reconciliation. The Sacrament of Penance and Reconciliation is the ceremony in which the faithful obtain absolution for sins committed against God and neighbors and are reconciled with the community of the Church. The sacrament of Penance is considered the normal way to be absolved from normal sin, and thereby freed from being condemned to hell. The pendulum had reached the extreme and was now more or less back to normal, a workable sacrament.

An interesting anecdote happened in October 1962. I was teaching a course called "Introduction to the Bible" at my alma mater College St. Louis. The college was still under the control of the Eudist's Fathers, therefore denominational. My students were in their late teens. Change was in the air and we could feel it, especially the students. We had animated discussions not only on the bible but even about the existence of God. Three of my students were proclaiming to be atheists, or at least agnostics. They generally disagreed with me and we had lively debates. They were respectful of my person and position for it was a confrontation of ideas and not of people. I enjoyed it immensely. They respected the rules of the college by attending mass, night prayers and of course my classes. They were not revolutionaries but interested and interesting students.

The Cuban Missile Crisis was then upon us. The Russian fleet was on its way to Cuba with missiles and possibly atomic bombs. President Kennedy addressed the nation giving Khrushchev his well-known ultimatum.

During those few days all and sundry were without mirth. All were fearful of adverse decisions with consequential dire results. Churches were filled for mass and prayers. There was a line of students for every priest hearing confession. On the second evening I met my three self-proclaimed atheist students in the line for confession and when I asked their intention, they told me: when close to death one changes their mind. They were living out the adage *there aren't any atheists in foxholes*. They now saw the priest as God's messenger to forgive sins. I realized a priest hearing confessions is not replacing God but is just a messenger of God telling sinners to go in peace.

Some priests refused absolution on a myriad of reasons – divorce or contraception just two of many, sensing the confessors were not sincere. I disagreed with them and never refused absolution. I always felt anyone coming to another human being confessing his or her sins and asking forgiveness had to be sincere. Why else would they go through such humiliation?

As my priesthood matured, I held many other disquiets about the archaic decrees and customs of the Church.

In 2,000 years the Church has had more years with married clergy than with celibate clergy.

Priests can have sex outside marriage, while preaching from the pulpit that it is a sin for their parishioners to have extramarital sex.

Lay parishioners can preach from the altar, but an erstwhile priest cannot.

The Church readily chastises errant parishioners while looking the other way with wayward priests.

The Church hierarchy seems more interested in protecting its power than in the welfare of its people.

Too often seminarian graduates lack formal accreditation fomenting innumerable problems when facing a highly educated parish, notwithstanding a priest chooses to take a lay existence.

Of these latter concerns, more will follow.

Chapter II

GENESIS

My name is Joseph Leo Theriault. I am an Acadian.
"Acadie" is a derivation from the Algonquian Micmac (Mi'kmaq First Nation) word rendered in French as "cadie," meaning a piece of land; generally a favorable connotation. The Acadians are the descendants of French colonists who in the early 17th and into the 18th centuries settled in what is now known as Eastern Canada's Maritime Provinces (Nova Scotia, New Brunswick, and Prince Edward Island), as well as parts of Quebec, and present-day Maine to the Kennebec River. Many of the colonists came from Brittany, the Gallic Provence in Northwest France; making Acadians genetically related to Scots, Irish and Welsh. They followed Samuel de Champlain, "Father of New France," who developed a habitation at Port-Royal, Acadia (Annapolis Valley, Nova Scotia) in 1605; the first permanent European settlement north of Florida.

Port-Royal served as the capital of Acadia until its destruction by British military forces in 1613. France relocated the settlement and capital five miles upstream on the south bank of the Annapolis River, the site of the present-day town of Annapolis Royal. Over the next half century the colonists cultivated and inhabited the land as far off as Grand-Pré, 75 miles to the northeast. This community was immortalized by Henry Wadsworth Longfellow's poem "Evangeline," published in 1847, re-counting the subjugation and deportation of the Acadians by the British Crown.

The Expulsion of the Acadians, also known as the Great Upheaval, the Great Expulsion, the Great Deportation and Le Grand Dérangement, was the forced removal by the British of the Acadian people. The Expulsion (1755–1764) occurred during the French and Indian War, the North American theatre of Europe's Seven Years' War, and was part of the British military campaign against New France.

Although the Acadians were geographically and administratively separate from the French colonies in modern-day Quebec, they did participate in various local operations against the British. Striking against these reprisals and fearful of an entente between the two factions, the British acted.

They did offer reprieve if the Acadians signed an unconditional oath of loyalty to become British subjects – this was refused fearing the possibility of male Acadians being committed to fight against France during wartime. This difficult situation was exacerbated by religious differences; the British monarch was head of the Protestant Church of England and the Acadians were Roman Catholic.

In the first wave of the expulsion Acadians were deported to other British colonies, primarily to the Thirteen Colonies of America. They weren't especially welcomed in New England because of their language, cultural differences and religion. The majority returned north by riding shank's mare to what is now New Brunswick. During the second wave, after 1758, they were deported to Britain and France, from where they migrated to Louisiana. Cajun is a colloquialism of Acadian (a-cade-jen).

Of the 14,100 Acadians in the region, approximately 11,500 were deported and thousands died in the expulsions – mainly from diseases and drowning when ships were lost.

I am the progeny of those that trekked north from New England to Ste. Anne, New Brunswick on the salmon laden St. John River. All was well until the American War of Independence gendered a new idiom, the United Empire Loyalists. In 1785 many Loyalists were sanctioned "our land" by the British Crown for their obvious loyalty. Our Ste. Anne became Fredericton, now the capital of New Brunswick. We were on the move again. The Ste. Anne Acadians traversed 150 miles northwest on the iconic river to Grand Falls in the area of Madawaska – Madawaska, Maine as well as New Brunswick.

After the War of 1812, we did not have to move again, but we were separated from our southern relatives by the newly established border dividing Madawaska New Brunswick from Madawaska Maine.

Chapter III

MY YOUTH

I was born in 1934 in Drummond, New Brunswick, Canada that is part of the Greater Madawaska region. The small village of Drummond is in rolling hills bordered by the Saint John River, Salmon River and Little River. It was and is the home to a proud francophone community living in a beautiful bucolic setting of rolling hills and serpentine rivers.

I remember my grandparents very well. My maternal grandfather was a rough carpenter who was a gregarious storyteller. His wife made the best donuts I have ever eaten and whenever I pass a Tim Horton's franchise the aroma wafting through the environ takes over my consciousness and I picture my grandparent's kitchen and my grandfather poking fun at my grandmother. Their youngest son, my uncle was younger than I. My paternal grandfather owned a gristmill on the Salmon River. His wife was rather cantankerous and the only peace in the house was when she had a cold or flu. My grandfather on this side of the table was just grim, more grouchy than garrulous.

My father had an opportunity to take over the mortgage of one of my great uncle's farmland in exchange for boarding him gratis in perpetuity. He lived for another five years and my father felt he got the poor end of the arrangement. I was the eldest of twelve and we assisted in working the farm from dawn to dusk; milking was at five A.M. and five P.M.. We preferred the winter months as our father worked the bush or the lumber camps, the fields were covered with snow and we attended school. My favorite of my mother's cooking were her pumpkin pies; I did and I still have a sweet tooth.

Three of my sisters became schoolteachers, one brother acquired and worked the farm, one an anthropologist, one a Canadian Customs inspector and yet another a contractor in Shawinigan. At time of writing nine of my siblings are still with us.

Due to the attrition of our people through forced emigration, European immigration and English domination we became more or less serfs on our own fields. Integration was difficult, political clout nonexistent. We Acadians were losing our identity, our culture and our language. To overcome this dilemma, Mother Church initiated *La Revanche du Berceau*, "the revenge of the cradle," an adage requiring little interpretation. English speaking families had only one or two children who often went off to college and alluring cities and never returned to their rural beginnings thus allowing for the relative economical purchase of their fallow land. The Revenge was often misconstrued as *solely* an exigency for the expansion of Catholicism, but it was also an act of survival for a people. The Church, of course, banned contraceptives thereby increasing the birth rate as well as did the "revenge."

To offset the French explosion, the political powers-to-be in the capital Fredericton, at this time primarily composed of the issue of United Empire Loyalists (UELs), offered much of the surrounding farmland to Irish immigrants who came to the area during the Great Irish Famine in the mid-nineteenth century. In addition, a quarter of a century later, the government augmented the UELs and Irish by colonizing our neck of the woods with Danes; New Denmark was established a few miles south of our community. Although the Danes leant themselves to the English language, the cultural offset was in general a failure because the Irish assimilated into the French community. The Irish also had their own cradle revenge against the English.

At the time of my birth the farming community of Drummond was completely French whereas the commercial town of Grand Falls, three miles from church to church, was completely Anglophone. Our parish, 300 families strong, consisted of 60 Acadian, 20 English speaking kinfolk and the remainder being Québécoise French.

Today, the greater community hosts Lutheran, Anglican, Roman Catholic, and Pentecostal churches. Its five major ancestries are: English (50.1%), French (36.4%), Danish (17.0%), Scottish (12.4%), and Irish (11.9%). The French language, however, is dominant; the cradle diktat prevailed.

The farm of my youth was comprised of only one hundred acres that meagerly supported our family of fourteen. We had a dozen or so dairy cows and sold the cream to the local creamery. We had chickens, pigs and sheep. The latter we sheared for wool and sold the lambs for cash. About half of our acreage was used for growing marketable potatoes and we had a small vegetable garden for our own consumption.

The local school was on our property and supported grades one through eight; one classroom and one lay teacher. There were, however, only a dozen or so students because most only wanted the ability to read and write, with a little math thrown in, before they went back to the land, the lumber camps, the sawmills, or pulp mills. The eldest boy was expected to take over the responsibility of the farm as the parents aged into semi-retirement status. No-one ever really retires from the labors of a family farm.

Being the eldest I was therefore expected to inherit the responsibilities of the farm. Going contrary to the hoi polloi, our parent's desired all of us acquire a high school education. Save for one, we did so accomplish.

English was not part of our school curriculum.

My future was molded by two events in my childhood that didn't surface for me until well into my maturity.

The first was my early birth only two months after my parents were married.

Abortion was a mortal sin and wasn't available even if contemplated. To be sent to remote cousins wasn't an option because our close-knit family didn't have any distant cousins. Off to a nunnery was a possibility but my grandfather wouldn't permit anything of the sort. My parents had to suffer the slings and arrows of their outrageous transgression. Our parish priest, Father Lévesque, was the first and foremost to sling mud and notch the bow.

The banns of marriage were the public announcement or proclamation by the priest at Mass to announce an impending marriage, enabling anyone to raise objection to the marriage if so committed. The banns were announced at three consecutive Masses.

As related to me by my grandfather two decades later, when the priest proclaimed the banns he admonished my parents; especially my mother. This was both his vindictive nature as well as his hope someone would cry out with an objection to the marriage. This was particularly damning as a few months prior he had appointed my mother the first president of the Children of Mary, an organization established to support the virginity of unwed mothers.

The diatribe came to a halt when my grandfather threatened to take our extended family from the parish. My grandfather said Father Lévesque ceased and desisted in his harangue, proving to be all thunder and no lightening; lightening being a reference to both enlightenment as well as action.

At my baptism grandfather said to Father Lévesque, "Should we baptize this thing or let it die?"

"Oh sir," said the priest, "How can you say such a thing? Of course, he'll be baptized and not only that, I will anoint him with a Special Blessing."

The favor of a Special Blessing was believed to be a gift, a gift of receiving, understanding and living Jesus' love.

My father accepting this reparation and forgave the priest for his unwarranted and untoward slanders; he even came to admire, trust and perhaps love him.

The second event that probably fashioned my adulthood occurred when I was but seven. Again, I didn't know or at least understand the episode as it occurred until decades later. The central figure of the drama was once again Father Lévesque.

Seven families approached the bishop in the Diocese of Bathurst, 140 miles to the northeast of Drummond, and accused their parish priest of molesting their sons; their sons were altar boys attending the sacrament of the Eucharist. This pronouncement rocked our unified community. Accusing the disciple of God of the most repugnant of activities, of iniquities incomprehensible, was both prestigious and prodigious. To condemn him of lust, child molestation and pedophilia was beyond the pale; unacceptable recklessness outside agreed standards of decency. The community was struck to its inner core and *those whom God hath joined together did go asunder.*

Father Lévesque was never placed on civil trial, never faced a Church synod or a Church tribunal but the bishop acted swiftly and with little mercy. The priest was shipped off to a Catholic hospital in Rivière-du-Loup, his hometown some 100 miles NW of Drummond, where he was forbidden to have any contact whatsoever with children. But a far more devastating punishment to a priest was his prohibition from performing the liturgical, theological and spiritual rites of the Catholic Church. For a priest to be unable to perform Mass, the sacrament of the Eucharist, is for a priest to reside in Purgatory on earth. He was in his early forties and had many decades to lament his pride and his sins.

My father did not believe in the abominations and remained with the cadre of believers in the Church, the priesthood and Father Lévesque. It was years after the rift that my father succumbed to the truth as presented to him by those who were victims of "the group of seven"; four of whom were my great uncles on my mother's side.

I fear I might have inherited the genes of my father – tolerance, denial and the convention of ignoring wrong or unpleasant events by turning the other way.

In rural New Brunswick the Roman Catholic Church was our lifeline; especially to French Canadians. The church was everything to the community. Beyond faith, it afforded stability, friendship, unity, support, and hope. The parish priest was our connection to the world at large as well as to God. Our political preference was thus dictated. The Church was the compass that directed all aspects of life – our faith, our salvation, our political counsel, our pleasure, our recreation, our community adhesion, our legal guidance, our comforter in days of strife or mourning – our day-to-day existence. On top of this pyramidal existence sat the parish priest. All the power of the Church hierarchy was in the hands of the local cleric and he generally wielded it with austere authority. He was loved, respected, feared but never questioned.

When I was young the priest was literally considered the father of the parish. Most problems were referred to him and his decisions were indisputable. He was highly respected, and his word was inviolable. He was the exemplar for adolescents and young adults. Most families felt blessed to have a priest in their family.

Religious instruction came from *le Catechisme du Quebec*, primarily based on the Old Testament rather than the New Testament. It preached the fear of God more than His love. Even the Ten Commandments were not a faithful translation of the original text; e.g. Premarital sex was a sin whereas the Commandments state: "Thou shalt not commit adultery" and "Thou shalt not covet thy neighbor's wife." Religions tend to become too ritualistic and the Roman Catholic Church is no exception. Ambiguity and fabrications are rife.

It was preached if one received Holy Communion on the first Friday of the month for nine consecutive months they were assured salvation; out of the church damnation. The "true truth" could only be found in the Catholic Church. The Pope is infallible. Jews are wicked because they killed Jesus. An infant dying before baptism cannot be buried in the cemetery because the baptismal ritual contains an exorcism section expelling the devil from the newborn. Divorcees cannot be buried in the cemetery. Those committing suicide cannot be buried in the cemetery. All unrighteous are buried in the field outside the fence. Sexual intercourse is the right of the husband and the duty of the wife. French kisses lasting only up to one minute are venial, forgivable, sins but over one minute becomes a mortal sin; the confessional, however, eradicates both.

Catholics distinguish between two types of sin. Mortal sins are a grave violation of God's law that turns man away from God. Someone who is aware of having committed mortal sins must repent having done so and then confess them in order to benefit from the sacrament. Venial sins, the kind that does not set us in direct opposition to the will and friendship of God, can be remitted by contrition and reception of other sacraments.

When a bootlegger's house burnt down when I was a boy the priest's sermon the following Sunday was on how God punishes evil. The following week the Rectory burnt down, and the homily was on how God tests his own.

These diktat examples are far from the Last Judgment message, "What you did to the least of mine you did unto me" and "love God above all and love your neighbor as yourself." These practices and teachings are but the tip of the proverbial iceberg and don't correspond to anything in the Gospel. Money, power and absurdity corrupt the supposed incorruptible – the clergy. The forthcoming Council Vatican II was sorely needed.

In my youth all families congregated daily to say the rosary. We attended mass on Sundays, but grandparents often attended daily. Holy days were celebrated with piety. God help the parishioner who fell negligent in his or her expected duties – duties being Mass attendance, the confessional, remuneration remittance, social contribution, sobriety, marital responsibilities, or avoidance of any of the Seven Deadly Sins of pride, greed, lust, envy, gluttony, wrath, and sloth – or any number of capricious whims of the parish priest. With so many potential moral failings, and the fear of the confessional, the priest had extraordinary and eternal power. The parish priest was considered the conduit to heaven and often mistaken as God incarnate or at the very least a demigod.

After mass, parishioners held a social of sorts on the church's porch. Newspapers were a rarity and radio reception was terrible so these gatherings were like the news hour we couldn't hear or a channel to local gossip. All and sundry reported the events of the week; horse trading, cattle prices, calving, new fandangle farm equipment, and of course politics always enlivened the assemblage.

My father apparently enjoyed these get-togethers as much as anyone and was usually the last to leave. It was reported Father Levesque attended as well as he certainly didn't want his flock to get out of hand or he to lose control. These socials were a great source of information that supplied material he could use in the pulpit.

The parish of Drummond was not a pious parish. Alcohol consumption was a commonality and it seemed every other house made beer or moonshine called "alcool"; spirits with up to 94% alcohol. It was so strong one had to use a mixer like 7-Up or ginger ale or it would evaporate before it reached their throat. Bootleggers liked to dilute the hooch and suspicious imbibers demanded a taste before purchase and if it didn't burn the tongue, they would take their business elsewhere. Some moonshiners went so far as to add lye to their diluted booze to ensure a zing to the taste. One of the parishioners died from drinking one of these lethal concoctions and at the funeral it was often related how Father Levesque knocked on the casket and said, "Emile, where did you get your booze? Ah, you got it at Charlie's. You should have known better." He continued with these antics until his uneducated, fallible, and superstitious disciples were trembling with fear; expecting Emile to jump out of his casket. It was a wonderful show of both wit and power.

Father Levesque was both revered and feared. In times of yore it was common practice for priests to call out the sins of individual parishioners from the pulpit and Father Levesque was not one to lose an opportunity to belittle his flock or stray from a useful instrument of supremacy.

One piece of gossip that showed his wit, of which he was not aware, was the story of Clara, a bootlegger of note. Seemingly on one occasion he told Clara to stop selling booze. She denied the avocation claiming spiteful rumors. He took her six-year-old boy aside for communion instruction and asked if hot water could be used for baptism. The boy responded to the negative because it would scald the baby.

"Can we use milk?"

"No, it is not water," the boy responded.

"Can we use booze"

"No, it is not water."

"How do you know?"

"Because Mom makes it."

Clara was scalded.

One Sunday he asked a parishioner what he intended to do with his crazy retarded son. The farmer responded, "It seems the only thing we can do with him is to send him to the seminary." Amazingly to the surprise of his faithful Father Levesque, who usually had a short fuse, burst out laughing. It appeared he appreciated strong backbones. Such responses also endeared him to many in his congregation.

I was but seven, attending instructions for confirmation, when Father Levesque was removed from the parish for pedophilia. I remember seeing him sitting on the rectory porch looking off into nowhere and appearing very sad. He was not allowed to see us nor we him. The parish was polarized. The seven who had complained to the bishop had been called out in the pulpit by Father Levesque and told they would go to hell. He called them individually by the seven deadly sins; Henri you are Wrath, Pierre you are Greed – he continued through sloth, pride, lust, envy, and gluttony. Henri's daughter later that week scratched her knee that bled. Almost immediately rumors spread she had been punished by God. That was the fear of the cloth and the ignorance of the people that persisted during my youth.

Two weeks later the bishop came to conduct our confirmation and instead of confirming us from the bishop's throne he sat in a straight chair out of the sanctuary – the space for the high altar and clergy.

It felt more like a funeral than a confirmation and the bishop rebuked us by saying this was what a parish looked like without a priest. He would send another priest and we had best try to accept him and work together.

Father Lévesque wrote his autobiography, but it was never published. An acquaintance, a friend of my sister, acquired snippets of the manuscript revealing his denial. Page 323 read:

> How many times in the middle of the night, especially during a full moon, did I walk through the graveyard, stop at a gravestone and pray. I would feel such relief, return to my room and was able to sleep. A full moon really affected me, and I seemed to become a totally different person with very strong sexual urges difficult to repress. I could generally control these compulsions through prayer and flagellation. I knew I had to repress my emotions at any cost. My inner demon, my inner voice, would take over my whole being; my language became very blunt and straight forward, "shut-up and do what I tell you."
>
> "Yet under that tough persona was hiding a very tender and emotional person. I was attracted to children, these preadolescents with such soft skin, but I could always control my emotions by limiting myself to only touching, caressing and fondling them – like a mother would, or like a father should. I always managed to resist the sexual attraction, even if the devil was tormenting me. Yes, I had urges but I always controlled them. I never molested any of them. I was accused of so doing but I never went overboard. They wanted to get the best of me. My assistant Gagnon was accusing me of these evil deeds while all the time I was thinking he was working for the common good of the parish. Although I know I should, I will never forgive him.

The bishop appointed Father Alfred Lang and the parish prospered under his tutelage and became one of the best in the diocese. He was the embodiment of what the Church expects of a priest. He was industrious, sympathetic, trustworthy and generous. What a difference between a priest like Lang and a priest who has sexual desires for children. Thank God we have many priests like him, priests who will most likely never make the headlines. As the saying goes, "good does not make noise, and noise is not always good, but shallow brooks are noisy." We should not expect more because this is our calling and the way of the Lord.

Father Lang's industry empowered the construction of a new community hall and a new high school where my brothers and sisters matriculated. Against the will of proud and tenacious farmers he brought in an agronomist to offer advice on soil management that forever left the farmers in his debt. Father Lang was the compassionate priest that secretly distributed condoms to his poor parishioners. All in the parish knew they could confide in and ask life direction of Father Lang, sans the confessional, and be confident the issue would not go further.

He also encouraged young boys to become priests, personally paying for their, and my, private education. One day of recollection Father Lang asked if I would like to attend high school at a new college in Edmundston. Each parish could sanction two students. Edmundston was but forty miles away but to me the moon seemed closer. I was honored, delighted and accepted, but my father was disappointed. He knew he was about to lose his heir apparent.

It was Father Lang's personal generosity that allowed me to attend this private school afar. Many years later, after my ordination, I asked if I could reimburse him for his financial help. He declined my offer but asked me to do unto others as he did for me. He not only preached Luke 6:31 – do unto others as you would have them do to you – but he so did live. This was reminiscent of Lloyd C. Douglas's novel and movie *Magnificent Obsession*. (Douglas had three other novels making it to the big screen; *The Robe, White Banners* and *The Big Fisherman*).

Father Lang's words inspired my priesthood for the rest of my life.

During the months of July and August 1947 my family and I did little else but prepare for boarding school; mentally as well as physically. We were all very excited, but I was too young to appreciate the immense life change forthcoming. An old trunk was filled with clothes and my mother sewed required name tags on every piece of clothing. I was anxious to go as I imagined a great adventure as well as a departure from the humdrum and laborious work of a family farm. I did have a tinge of pride as I was one of only two to be chosen by our priest and perhaps even the bishop to attend a private school. As September approached, however, the fear of the unknown became palpable. The reality of leaving my six younger siblings (five were yet to be born), my parents, my friends, and the commonality of life, appeared insurmountable. My bravado for the unknown was waning. My bragging rights were worthless. My ventures thus far were limited to a week or two at my grandparents only a few miles from our farm and now I was off to the unknown.

When the day of departure arrived, my father drove me to the church to meet Father Lang who was to drive my classmate Candide and me to the college. When leaving home, barely able to look over the door panel of the huge Plymouth due to being of challenged height; I viewed our entire family waving frantically as if enjoying a parade. My mother then broke away as tears began to flow; her baby was leaving home far too soon. I rubbed my eyes with the back of my fists as I didn't want Father Lang, and especially my fellow student, see I had been crying.

On our way to Edmundston, Candide and I were sitting in the back seat, mostly mute because we were not close friends and we were both terrified. Father Lang attended to the ride on the terrible dirt road and refrained from chitchat. I was but thirteen weighed barely 70 pounds and the immensity of our adventure was rapidly sinking in and I was already homesick.

Chapter IV

SCHOOL DAYS

The Edmundston campus I was to attend was known as Collège Saint-Louis. It was founded by the Apostolic Order of Eudist Fathers in 1946 as a school for boys to receive a classical education. The Congregation of Jesus and Mary was instituted at Caen, in Normandy, France in 1643 by Saint Jean Eudes, an exemplar of the French school of spirituality. The principal works of the Congregation are the education of priests in seminaries and the giving of missions.

I was to be a charter member of the school.

Camaraderie among the 35 of us was immediate because we were all in the same boat – we were very young, new to the environment and all a bit homesick. Electricity hadn't reached the homes of rural Canada in the mid-40s but our church had incandescent lighting as did the stores and homes in Grand Falls consequently I was not unduly amazed at our dormitory lighting, but indoor plumbing was a wholly different matter. I was both bewildered and traumatized by the porcelain bowls because I didn't know how to flush them.

Being a new school had its good points because we were all novices and didn't have to go through the humiliation of upper classmen hazing neophytes. Indoctrinating events did occur, although minimally, in years to come. A close restraint was held by the Eudist Fathers. A few of the "big city" boys tried to rule it over us country bumpkins but it didn't last when classes got underway as it soon became apparent we were as academically acute as they, and they were as ingenuous as we.

The school was probably unlike most schools in Canada at the time. For starters, it was boys only. Additionally, we were quartered in World War II army barracks while a new college campus was under construction. These facilities were single story, shaped like an "H" with the heating components, washbasins, showers, and toilets in the cross bar. The uprights held the dormitories and another H-Hut was used for classrooms. The cafeteria was in an old administration building and the meals were generally good, but boring. Breakfast was another matter. Breakfast consisted of porridge, porridge and more porridge; oatmeal for the uninitiated. Heating was by date and not by climate. Forty degrees Fahrenheit on June 1st made little matter as the rules stated furnaces were to be turned off May 31st. The heating system lacked efficiency in the first place and many a day we wore mittens in the classrooms. Save for one lay teacher, the faculty was comprised of priests; about a dozen. Again, unlike other Canadian schools our studies consisted mainly of Latin, Greek, religion, French literature, mathematics, ancient history, and a smattering of English. The Eudist's differed from other orders by opening their doors to all comers and not solely those considering joining the order. They therefore limited religious studies to only a couple classes weekly. We did, however, have Mass every morning and vespers every evening; reveille was at six A.M. and lights-out at nine P.M..

We were kept busy during the days as our instructors strongly believed in the adage that an idle mind is the devil's playground. Days were fun but nights were difficult as loneliness slowly but assuredly crept in. Lights-out induced whispers, gossips and giggles but then the enveloping blackness opened the doors and windows to the invasion of bogeymen. My rosary kept me company until I succumbed to the sandman. I always kept it under my pillow and it saved me from falling too deeply into melancholy; I missed my sisters and brothers more than I could ever have imagined. At home lights-out meant great laughter, frolicking and pillow fights.

Lights-out now meant complete silence, or supposedly so.

I often laid awake remembering life on the farm. Getting up at five in the morning to milk cows was a disagreeable chore but I would have done it now in a heartbeat. I could almost smell mom's breakfast of eggs and beans and buckwheat pancakes; the pancakes were like leavened Mexican tortillas. We had real maple syrup. We kids tussled about the table but we ate every morsel. The buckwheat flour came from my grandfather's gristmill and was considered the best in our county, and beyond. Buckwheat shells were piled behind the mill and we loved to play in the fluffy pile. It was like frolicking in a snow bank that was warm. The shells were a good home insulation except if you had a rat or knothole whereby the shells would pour out like water.

Almost every night I pined for my three brothers and three sisters and wondered if they missed me as much as I did they. Often to enable slumber I reviewed the classes of the day. Latin grammar was a challenge but in these early days I had a photographic memory and by the end of my second year I had memorized the Latin grammar from cover to cover, even the punctuations and page numbers.

Boys will be boys and lights out silence was not always respected. If the supervisor was late or had to leave to answer the phone or whatever we would take advantage of his absence and play tomfoolery. A case in point occurred during my second year. Our "H" hut dormitories had 30 army cots in each upright separated by a hall. One evening our supervisor was absent and the supervisor of the other dorm had to oversee both wings. After he retired, we felt safe for horseplay. To secure our freedom two students tied a rope to two beds in his wing that he would have to traverse to reach us. It worked; we had fun for about 30 minutes and then the unfortunate priest, upon hearing our ruckus, awoke, tripped on the rope and gave us the warning we deserved. Fortunately for him, and for us, he was not badly injured. That is not saying, however, his self-esteem and our future freedom were not badly battered.

School helped me a great deal with loneliness and I was a good student. We had monthly report cards and the first month I came in 6th out of a class of 23, the second month 4th, the third month 3rd which I maintained until May, when I led the class.

In mid-October I was walking among the barracks when I saw my dad's old Plymouth. What a wonderful surprise. He was in town on business with a friend and could only stay a short time, but a short time I relished. It was only a 40 mile drive from home but in those days and in our milieu it was like light years away. It was a good thing he didn't come a few weeks earlier for I would definitely have gone home with him.

Sports were limited. We had a small softball field and an outdoor hockey rink that's upkeep was the student's responsibility. We especially enjoyed flooding the rink as it was done at night and was a welcome break from the books and general monotony. Also, as a bonus we were allowed to sleep in the following morning. We had admittance to an old army drill hall that was perfect for basketball – a sport I loved. My height was a deterrent for greatness, but I loved it just the same. I couldn't afford the equipment, so hockey was out of the question. I was one of the smallest in my class until our fourth year when I had a growth surge and caught up physically to my classmates.

Our temporary campus was close to downtown, but we seldom ventured off grounds. When we so did we had to go in groups; not for safety but for preventing errant behavior. We went to the odd hockey game and a few movies. We particularly loved Bud Abbot and Lou Costello movies. We did have movies in the drill hall, but they were mostly nature documentaries from the National Film Board of Canada. We did see, but not heard, old silent movies like the original 1925 *Ben Hur* and a lot of Charlie Chaplin slapstick movies. We were probably shown silent movies because suitable French movies were unavailable. Personal radios were a luxury of the future, but we could listen to the school's radio on special days off, usually offered to us by a snowstorm or a visit by the bishop. We played cards, board games and chess was particularly popular.

Listening to Saturday's Hockey Night in Canada was a highlight of the week and almost to a boy we rooted for the Montreal Canadiens.

Our letters were always opened as was common in French boarding schools. This did not bother us but on one occasion the practice got a few of us in serious trouble.

One of the priests had his favourites for whom he gave special treatment; early vacation departure or special permission to go into town. We happened upon a letter from one favorite's girlfriend and adolescently altered it and returned it to the girl. The letter said he was skating without a hat, a naked head in French, and we erased the "head."

Among our additions or alterations we wrote "censored by Blagdon." We did not put Reverend or Father since that priest had a brother in our class and in our naivety, we thought we were safe by just using the name, Blagdon. If the joke back fired we could say we meant the student and not the priest. The girl's family was friends of the rector and Father Blagdon, and they sent the letter to the rector with unfavorable comments. We were in trouble. Fecal matter hit the rotating impeller.

The rector came in our classroom and reprimanded the entire class by saying Father Blagdon was the holiest of all his priests. He gave orders to the Director of Discipline to root out the culprits and threatened expulsion. There were seven of us involved; one supplied the envelope, one supplied the stamp, one supplied the pen and the other four wrote the comments.

For an unknown reason the rector wanted the boy who actually mailed the letter and two days later the Director of Discipline called five of us to his office. We didn't know why he picked five and not the entire seven. We were too scared to figure one of the two absent was likely the squealer. He again threatened expulsion for the boy who actually mailed the letter. He pointed his finger at four of us in turn and asked if we mailed the letter. We stuck together and denied the action. He skipped the boy who was the perpetrator.

We left his office knowing full well he knew who the felon was yet he let him and the rest of us off the hook. To this day I hold a great admiration for this man.

My parents visited occasionally but of course the highlights of the year were holidays at home for Christmas, Easter and summer vacations; I never complained of laboring in the fields or the muck of the barns and sties again.

One distressing event for a boy of thirteen occurred when I became ill in my first year. It was either a bad cold or the onset of influenza. Nonetheless, I went to the infirmary to consult the nurse – a priest. He told me I had a terrible cough and brought forth a tongue suppressor. He asked me to lower my pants and when he checked my throat, he fondled my testicles.

I brought this news to my class proctor and spiritual advisor and shortly thereafter the nurse disappeared from campus.

After two years in the military barracks we moved into the new college high on a hill overlooking the city. It was the pride of Edmundston. It was to have a campus with appropriate college grounds, but it was still under construction. Jack hammer and other construction noises were unremitting. We perpetually ate and breathed sawdust and concrete dust. The exterior grounds were an array of building material, but we were as happy as magpies. We had a proper gym, a standard sized hockey rink, a chemistry lab, a library with room to study, and a modern cafeteria. But alas, a continuum of the detested breakfast porridge. We augmented breakfasts with peanut butter and Ritz crackers which became a staple we hoarded. There was a commissary of sorts selling soft drinks, peanuts and chocolate bars.

The student body increased from our meager 35 live-ins and 20-day students to 500; the 500 was more or less divided evenly between live-ins and day students. A good number of students now came from the Province of Québec and we comingled splendidly save for a few that came from Québec City and relative wealth. The latter group were arrogant and tried to intimidate us, but were mostly ignored.

After three years in high school we were deemed to be at the provincial level of grade twelve, but I continued at Collège Saint-Louis for another four years. In my second year we could go to town Sunday afternoons without supervision and, beyond belief, in years three and four we were allowed to go twice a week until the unbelievable hour of 9:30.

During these years leading to my Bachelor of Arts degree I considered careers in medicine, law, agronomy, veterinary – but the priesthood kept calling. I was not pressured by the Church nor my family to choose a secular life but serving the Catholic community appealed to me. The priesthood was a most honorable and respected vocation within the French-Canadian commonwealth.

I considered the ministry as a helping profession. The parish priest in small rural French communities was considered as an all-encompassing individual, bordering on the omnipotent. Beyond being the spiritual guidance, the priest was the doctor, the lawyer, the teacher, and the accountant.

Two of my teachers were influential; Father Raoul Martin who intervened in the nurse situation and Father Cotreau, my math teacher, who loved his profession and was always there for advice and guidance greatly appreciated by a teenager entering adulthood and probing for knowledge.

Father Raoul Martin was a very special man and influenced me greatly. He was the Academic Director, our homeroom teacher and our professor of Latin. He was small, about 5' 4," and had a limp due to childhood polio. He always seemed happy and made learning a pleasure. As mentioned, by the end of my second year I knew the entire Latin grammar by heart. God knows I hated and struggled with French and English grammar. He was impartial, empathetic and always had time to help. We nicknamed him "Ti-Jeff," little Jeff, from the comic characters "Mutt and Jeff."

In our third year of school we had a professor who graduated summa cum laude in his mathematics' master's degree from Laval University. He may have been an excellent mathematician, but he lacked a modicum of teaching skills. It wasn't long before we started taking advantage of this weakness and disrupted the class by asking innocuous but distracting questions. It was great fun, a diversion from daily tedium but we were not learning anything. Two of us took it upon ourselves to self-teach one another and we took pertinent questions to the master. This got us through, but it did not save the teacher and he was gone the following year.

It was the following year we were blessed by Father Cotreau, the new math professor. He was a six foot, 200-pounder with good teaching skills and a no-nonsense attitude. He was soft spoken, was nobody's fool, objective, and always ready to help. No more shenanigans, but significantly improved learning. The following year we were sanctioned to double occupancy sleeping quarters and Father Cotreau was our supervisor. It was a great improvement over the previous dormitory and the supervisor with his favorites.

Perhaps it was expected of me to enter the priesthood but as implied earlier I was never inveigled to so do so by my family or the faculty. I was attracted and not forced to priesthood. The attraction was a call of duty, a call of service to help my fellow man. At this tender age the lure of authority was also in the amalgam. All concerned were very pleased by my choice of calling and my parents were extremely proud.

I was at *Collège Saint-Louis* in Edmundston from the age of 13 in 1947 to 1954. I was an "A" student and always in the top ten percent of the class. I graduated with a Bachelor of Arts degree at the age of twenty. I was president of my class; I was valedictorian and I was off to a seminary in Québec City.

Chapter V

THE SEMINARY

When I registered with the bishop to become a diocesan priest, he directed me to the Grand Seminary at Laval University in Quebec City. I was to study for my master's in divinity. A diocesan priest is a Catholic, Anglican or Eastern Orthodox priest who commits himself or herself to a certain geographical area and is ordained into the service of the citizens of a diocese, a church administrative region.

Université Laval is a French language, public university in Québec City. It began in 1663 by Francois de Montmorency-Laval as a seminary, thereby making it the oldest center of higher education in Canada and the first North American institution to offer higher education in French. The modern university was founded by royal charter issued by Queen Victoria in1852, and is presently ranked among the top ten Canadian universities in terms of research funding. Notable graduates include three Prime Ministers, eight Quebec Premiers and eleven Supreme Court Justices. Present student population is 32,000 undergraduates and 11,000 postgraduates.

When I reached Laval University seminary campus I was to be the 72nd class to graduate since inauguration. It was my first year in higher university, but I felt I had been sequestered most of my young life.

Our twig of the large campus tree of Laval was cloistered literally as well as figuratively. We kept to our own back yard in spirit as well as body. We heard the raucous interchange common on all university campuses driving us further into prayer. Fortunately for us as well as our mentors, coeducation had yet to reach Canadian campuses – especially French, Roman Catholic campuses. As we wandered about grounds, we surreptitiously glanced their way while they openly stared at us; we in full black cassocks must have appeared as maladroit aliens. We may have at time secretly envied them and their joyful way of life, but we sensed the feelings were not mutual. We did have God on our side, and we were sure we would prevail.

Until my directive the majority of French priests did not hold a bachelor's degree, let alone a Masters. Four years of university education without accreditation was considered to be humble. It might have appeared to be virtuous, but it became a burden for those who later decided to leave the priesthood without holding any form of academic degree or credentials.

Not only was it difficult for priests to attain occupation in "civvy street," but it was a great burden upon retirement, especially in the United States. The Society of Jesus, the Jesuits, may be considered an elite order in Roman Catholicism with goals of higher education, creative and systematic work to increase the stock of knowledge, and cultural pursuits. A known Jesuit priest, professor at Loyola University in Chicago, had a major drinking problem. He was given many opportunities and treatment for his lifestyle reversal but all to no avail. This man of culture, education and religious attainment was ousted from the order. As he had never paid into the US social security system nor had any pension from the order, he was broke and bereft of income opportunity. At the age of 62, he became a bag boy at a grocery store on Woodward Avenue in Detroit.

Bishop Gagnon of Edmundston had greater forethought than most at the time by wanting his clerics to be at least as well educated as their modern flock. There were 80 students my first year and the manuals were mostly in Latin. Most of the seminarians were from Québec but there were also scholars from South Korea, Panama, Venezuela, the United States, and English Canada. The Anglophones came to learn French, but many ended up teaching English to the Francophiles instead of learning French.

At Grand Seminary we were exposed to a very strict discipline. Up at 5:30 in the morning and rigorously scheduled for the whole day until 9:30 P.M.; half an hour of meditation preceded mass that preceded breakfast that preceded an hour reading breviary, our book of prayers. We had theology classes all day. It was as though we were in a monastery with prayers before and after meals, evening prayers at Chapel, prayers ad infinitum.

Oddly enough the most influential facet of my seminarian education was communism or, better said, anti-communism.

During these years Communism was in full bloom and its influence was worldwide. Bulgaria, Czechoslovakia, East Germany, Poland, Hungary, Romania and the Baltic States were under the yoke of Russian Marxism-Leninism. China, North Vietnam, North Korea, and Laos were soon to follow as was Cuba, Venezuela and Chile.

Unbeknown to our cloistered French environ, anti-communism was running rampant in the United States and elsewhere in Western Europe. We were unaware of McCarthyism, the John Birch Society or Father Charles Edward Coughlin of radio infamy – but we had our own influence. Our fear was not of the bizarre economic ranting of Karl Marx, but of the atheistic accompaniment of these tenets.

Our fears were well within the realm of reality. The working class of Québec was dominated and subjugated by the provincial government of Maurice Duplessis. Although he was anti-communist and pro-education, he was vehemently opposed to trade unions. This was our fear, an uprising of the proletariat against Duplessis' iron fist and a consequential backlash against Christianity, and for us Catholicism.

At the time there were over 100,000 lumbermen in Québec, a small army, eking out a subsistence that was ripe for the Marxist movement. Leaflets and magazines, in French but post scripted *Pravda Moscow*, flooded the camps like so many tree leaves.

The Church decided to combat the heretical canons of communalism by assisting the oppressed in a manner slightly similar to socialism – trade unionism. Forefront in the battle was Bishop Gérard-Marie of Saint-Jean-de-Québec who said, "Mind your own business, but mind it."

During the early sixties Catholic Church attendance in France was in steep decline. In an attempt to stem the outward flow of parishioners, the dioceses adopted a form of Christian Socialism. It was called *Le Mouvement des Prêtres-ouvriers*, or "The Movement of Workers' Priests." The movement placed parish priests in the workforce enabling a closer, realistic association with their working parishioners.

The knowledge of this movement was opening a new dimension in French Canada as well. A Priest-Chaplin was assigned to each lumber camp, many living on-site, who offered more than the fantasy that was communism. They gave hands-on advice and with political clout and collective bargaining were able to improve money, hours and conditions. They demonstrated Christianity was far superior to humanism. It worked. The Church was a major factor, if not the main factor, in defeating communism in Québec and Canada.

Three of the ministers who were pivotal in this class struggle were Fathers Louis O'Neil, Father Gerard Dion, and Bishop Gustave Prevost.

Abbes Dion and O'Neill published a book titled *Le Chrétien et les Elections* (The Christian and the Elections) denouncing the antidemocratic manipulation of the elections by Premier Maurice Duplessis. This was an extremely valiant endeavor as Duplessis not only ruled the province but, to a large extent, the Church of Québec.

Change was in the air and our professors welcomed the movement. Most were progressive conservatives to moderate liberal and the struggle against communism was an evolution rather than a revolution. None were true radicals because it was not in the Church's disposition to either comprehend or sanction such a transformation.

Prevost had been a Bishop in China and was incarcerated by the Chinese Communist Government. Upon his release from prison he returned home to Québec to enlighten the public at large as to the true evils of communism. He was emaciated as Christ on the cross and his eyes were those of a caged animal. He worried Canada was heading towards communism and told us we had to be willing to face prison or death for our Faith.

"May your prison cell be more comfortable than mine. You may not be treated as badly as me, but it will still be a prison, nonetheless. You will have to answer for your faith as the signs are all there."

It was such a challenge for men so young that some even left the seminary. Communism was not just a concept but a reality in our backyard. For some of us it was a challenge we were willing to face. We were in our twenties and ready for action. We felt the best way to fight communism was to organize the lower classes and elevate them to middle class.

We had a Hungarian professor. He was a private secretary to a Cardinal when the communists overran his country. The Cardinal ordered his priests to flee the country and our professor barely made the escape. During one lecture he opined less than 20% of the Hungarian population were communist, and in the ignorance of youth we berated him for anyone allowing 20% of the population dictating to the remaining majority.

I will always remember his response, "I see 80 of you sitting there. If I had a machine-gun and I shot the first of you who stood, I assure you the remaining 79 will remain seated."

As stated, Communism greatly influenced my development as a young priest. We were continually harangued about its pandemic tactics of propaganda, infiltration and terror; encouraging the struggle between the classes by using the old Roman saying *Divide et Impera* (divide and conquer). The testimony of Bishop Prevost showed us the reality of communism. The literature gathered in lumber camps of Quebec showed us communism was diligently at work in Canada and especially in the "Catholic Province of Quebec."

The communists made the same mistake as did the United States during the War of 1812 by thinking French Canadians would do anything to throw off the yoke of British influence. In both incidences French Canada feared more the potential loss of their autonomy, their language and their religion.

In 1957, when Russia put its Sputnik in orbit, we were crestfallen. The Seminary was likened to a funeral home. Communist Russia was #1 and to add to our fear and humiliation they beat Team Canada in hockey.

We fought, however, and we won. The success of the Church in combating communism had positive results for years to come. Not only did it defeat communism, increase the financial well-being of the plebs, but it strengthened the Church in faith … and in parishioners.

Amen *omnibus, qui.*

The courses I took over the next four years included Latin, Hebrew, Theology, the Philosophy of St Thomas of Aquinas, the Trinity, history of the Church, Canon Law, Liturgy, and Spirituality – but zero science. We also studied Mariology, the theological study of Mary, the mother of Jesus. Mariology aims to connect scripture, tradition and the teachings of the Church on Mary. In the context of social history, Mariology may be broadly defined as the study of devotion to and thinking about Mary throughout the history of Christianity. We touched upon morality as a part of Aristotle's philosophy a la Aquinas.

Saint Thomas Aquinas (1225-1274) was an Italian Dominican friar and Catholic priest. He was an immensely influential philosopher, theologian, and jurist in the tradition of scholasticism; scholasticism being the attempt to bridge the gap between religion and reason.

These courses prepared us for the teaching of the testaments, the canons of the church, the confessional, but little else. We had tomes of theoretical teachings of Aquinas, in Latin, but scant pages on sexuality.

We were admonished to be careful, not to become activists nor get involved in politics – save for communism; we were to solely keep to the spiritual aspects of life. Science was not even considered because the bible teaches one how to get to heaven and not how the universe works; the difference between paradise and the sky. Render unto the scientists the things that are of science and unto God the things that are God's. The bible is for salvation.

Our studies were for us to understand and follow the doctrines of Jesus and to emulate his teachings as best we could. In times of need we were to reflect, "What would Jesus do in this situation; what would He do if he were in my place, under these conditions?" We were to preach upon and do onto others as you would have them do to you.

That said, however, the bible wasn't taken or taught literally. It was considered an extrapolation of Christ's parables; an allegorical or symbolic interpretation. The Seminary's approach might be considered hermeneutic – the philosophy and methodology of text interpretation; in our case, the interpretation of the bible.

Taking the bible literally opens the door for confusion because the gospels are not only ambiguous but are contradictory. Additionally, the gospels can be precast to the interpreters' interests that was – a very dangerous approach indeed. This fear of ambiguity is the antithesis of the assuredness of the so-called "born again" Christians.

The change in the Catholic Church from the literal to the interpretive was a relative new position. The splitting of the atom and Sputnik may have rushed the approach that was fomenting since Darwin's *Theory of Evolution*. We were taught evolutionary philosophy did not take away the power of God but increased it through the evolutionary *process.*

Classes on Aquinas were conducted as a study of logic. It was a "why" procedure designed to achieve the truth of the faith as well as the verification of the doctrine of the true Church. Aquinas' offerings were deemed to be both momentous and prophetic. Ask "why" five times and you have a good chance of reaching the real answer.

The small booklet on sexuality was transcribed primarily as a guidebook for the confessional and not as a manual to address the problems that would arise in the real world. This, in my mind, was and is a monumental schism in the education of seminarians.

Celibacy was taught in the context of abstinence from sexual intercourse. This was congruent to congregations having the vows of poverty, obedience and chastity; chastity being the practice of abstinence from sex for pleasure or for moral tenets. I felt I was sacrificing a sexual pleasure for a higher cause; like an athlete going through hard training for the satisfaction of being competitive. It was probably the same for other seminarians but several years after ordination many priests cavalierly changed their opinions on chastity feeling it wasn't suitable for the reality of life, the real world. They therefore interpreted celibacy in the narrow sense of restriction from marriage and not a constraint from sexual participation. They also reasoned diocesan priests didn't take the vow of chastity, only the vow to refrain from marriage, allowing them the freedom of a sensual life. This was obviously a very broad and liberal interpretation of our vows; an interpretation that often led to tragedy.

I read the book *Jesus at My Age* by Jordan A. Cook. This book became my mentor. When confronted with a quandary I attempted to imagine what Jesus would have said or done in a similar situation. Jesus became a friend I could relate to and rely upon. My spirituality was being transferred from the instructions of the Church to the teachings of Christ. What an uplifting transformation.

In early Christianity when a congregation needed a priest, they would elect a person they felt was best suited for the job and then got approval from the apostles or their representatives. With time monasteries began opening. The monks dedicated their lives to prayer and made the vows of poverty, chastity and obedience. They gave their rights, their worldly goods and chattels, to the congregation and received protection in return. Monks specialized in different fields such as scripture translation, printing, agriculture, wine making, and even liqueur distillation such as Chartreuse or Benedictine. Each monastery had one member satisfying priestly duties for the congregation and particularly good orators were invited to preach at different churches throughout the area. Some monks were offered the position of congregational priest and they would, understandably, carry with them their monastic foundation and influence. Eventually their influence affected the formation of parish priests in seminaries.

For four years seminarians lived a quasi-monastic life of prayer and meditation. This structure continued for centuries. Worldly activities were repudiated in favor of prayer and in my world we were told to beware of Sunday evenings after vespers when the loneliness of celibacy would be most prevalent.

Early in my seminary life I read the book *When My Life Becomes a Prayer*. It is a very simple approach. When one becomes aware that it is a loving God who makes all happen in the world and that we as individuals are powerless then our life becomes one of prayer. Archimandrite (head of a large monastery or honorary title given to a monastic monk) "Vasileios of the Iveron Monastery" on Mount Athos said, "When one spiritually matures, when one recognizes his own powerlessness and the ineffable love of God, one becomes calm and everything proceeds on its own. If you feel weak, you must give everything and entrust everything to God." There is an analogy with Alcoholic Anonymous' Serenity Prayer: "God, grant me the serenity to accept the things I cannot change, courage to change the things I can, and wisdom to know the difference." Our challenge is to deal with the struggles of life and in such a way as we gain humility and realize the love of God. Once we see His love and power, we will have a life filled with peace no matter what is happening around us. I believe helping a person in need is a prayer. Spreading good – compassion, inspiration, morality – around you is a prayer. If I had to choose between the breviary and helping someone in need, I would choose to help the person in need.

At last on June 29, 1958 the Big Day arrived and it didn't come any too soon for my liking. I was tired of the intellectual life and wanted to apply my education to practical purpose. I was but twenty-four but felt I had a lot to offer the world. After all, I had a master's degree in divinity and was wise beyond any age. I was also tired of the restrictions and often childish procedures of the seminary.

Two were to be ordained from the small parish of St Michel de Drummond and fifteen had preceded us. It was a big celebration for our families and for the parish. Not realizing things past, I asked Father Lévesque to preach at my first mass. He at first accepted but later sent his condolences and congratulations begging poor health. Of course, the reality was the bishop forbade him to come. I was still left in the dark about events of my birth and the Group of Seven.

My first appointment was professor of mathematics at College St-Louis, my Alma Mater. I was entering the world of academe and was to assist parish priests on weekends. After eight years of dormitory and cafeteria living, I was free with a modicum of responsibility at last.

Chapter VI

ONE TOO MANY

I was feeling very snug and a bit smug in my new position at the University; after all it was only four years since I was a student therein. I had my own bedroom, albeit closer to a broom closet in size – but it was mine – all mine. Leaving the seminary and getting into the work force was a welcome relief. I was now working in the master's vineyard and I knew without a doubt I was not made for monastic life.

I was a pretty good mathematician, so I felt comfortable at the front of the class facing the students. My Roman collar helped, but I was just a few years older than my students, so knowledge won the day. On the weekends I temped for local parish priests who were sick, on sabbatical or just needed a respite from the weekly grind. Celebrating Mass was the highlight of these ventures. When time permitted, I loved to go trout fishing or deer hunting and the occasional foray after moose and black bear.

During my first year of tutorials I was approached by an officer in the Canadian army. Major Boucher was from my hometown parish and was a priest in the Royal Canadian Army Chaplin Corp (RCAChC) and was based in Camp Petawawa, 110 miles (170 Km) northwest of the capital Ottawa. He asked if I would like to join the army in a militia position to sub for padres taking summer leave. I jumped at the opportunity.

When spring semester finished in 1959, I was off to the army with the rank of captain. It was extremely humiliating as I had never previously been in uniform, I had never taken basic training as had all of the other officers, and my English was deplorable. The redeeming dynamic was pay parade; I earned more money in two months than I did the remaining ten as a university professor. I was able to purchase my first car; a VW Beetle.

I spent a fair amount of time in the Officer's Mess and the camaraderie was wonderful. The other officers treated me as an equal as far as rank allowed and I did not receive the animosity I expected. It was a challenge because of my naivety, my youth, the restricted education I received at the seminary, and of course my limited English.

A major requirement of my position was to celebrate Mass every Sunday. The Mass or Eucharist is the central act of divine worship in the Catholic Church. The Eucharist, also called Holy Communion or the Lord's Supper, is considered a sacrament. The Catholic Church recognizes seven sacraments: Baptism, Confirmation, Eucharist, Reconciliation (Penance or Confession), Anointing of the Sick, Marriage, and Holy Orders (ordained bishops, priests and deacons).

Besides the Eucharist, I was expected to perform the other sacraments. I did visit the sick at the base infirmary as well as the hospital in the town of Petawawa. Since Canada hadn't been at war since the Korean Conflict seven years past, I did not have to worry about or spiritually treat soldiers suffering from Post-Traumatic Stress Disorder (PTSD). My major concern was that my naivety didn't negatively affect the soldiers and their families.

In hindsight, however, I fear my innocence might have betrayed at least one family.

One of the parishioners approached me with allusions of sexual abuse within the Catholic community; in fact, pedophilia. I, at least, perceived them to be innuendos. She conveyed her fear of horrendous events taking place at a particular time, a particular place and on numerous occasions. She asked me to investigate. I told her I would have to report it to my superior officer Major Boucher. She became quite upset at this disclosure and asked me to reconsider. I explained I had no choice but to take it higher on the chain of command. She left with a distraught demeanor.

I reported the conversation to Major Boucher but upon request I didn't identify the woman. This was the last I heard of the incident and thought the woman was over distraught or the major nipped the problem in the bud.

In 1995 General Boucher's sister died whereby he celebrated the Mass and gave the sermon. The liturgical problem was at this time he was waiting for a court date for having sexually molested altar boys. His apparent victims had blackmailed him into giving them money from the church's coffers. As a counteraction they were brought to court and General Boucher was the Crown's main witness. He testified the defendants blackmailed him because they claimed he molested them when they were altar boys. They were found guilty and sentenced to prison.

Twenty-three years after Camp Petawawa, at the age of 73, Brigadier General Boucher was finally accused of sexually abusing minors. During the procedure some friends and classmates of his said he was molesting altar boys immediately after his ordination. He had apparently been abusing minors for over 40 years before he got caught. Because of his age and ill health, he was placed on house arrest at a convent where he could still celebrate Mass but could not have any association with minors. He died at the age of 81.

In retrospect, I feel the lady at Camp Petawawa was trying to tell me it was Major Boucher who was sexually abusing minors. If I hadn't been so naïve, hadn't so adulated the major, and of course know what I do today, events might have turned out differently and certainly for the better. How many lives had he ruined in the interim because of my naivety?

Chapter VII

FARMERS ASSOCIATION

A bout this time in my life I realized there were two classes of priests in our diocese, those who were self-caring and those who were flock caring. The Sunday collections were for the administration of the parish and the rectors were paid by tithing. Each fall after crops were harvested and livestock butchered the priest would make his calls on each parishioner to collect his due stipend. Rectors of a rich parish were relatively well-off financially. They usually had the best car in the parish and were coveted by many priests from less endowed communities. My native parish was one of means and our priest drove a magnificent Buick Electra 225. He went to the extreme of naming-out delinquent tithe payers from the pulpit. This was most embarrassing for all parishioners, especially the offenders who often could ill afford the money.

Besides the rich parishes, there were middle-class and poor parishes and the rectors lived accordingly. Rector Assistants were paid $50.00 a month plus room and board; even if they were in a rich parish. Only rectors could own a car and it was not uncommon to see a rector drive by in a Chrysler New Yorker followed by an assistant on his bicycle. Some assistants would buy a car, register it in a relative's name and say it was only borrowed; childish but effective. It was apropos as many rectors treated their assistants as children even going as far as establishing nightly curfews.

Parishioners were largely generous to their priests. In addition to the tithe, priests had free admittance to concerts, movie theatres, plays, family dinners, and even at some restaurants. Dental and medical services were free. Priests were not rich, but neither were they poor.

A Franciscan missionary, Father Firmin Lachapelle, ministered a very poor mission parish about ten miles from my grandfather's gristmill at Salmon River, New Brunswick. Each spring he would ask my grandfather for a calf he would feed all summer to butcher in the fall. My grandfather would deliver the calf by wagon with a good supply of oats. Many families did likewise for Father Firmin and other poor parishes and were very happy to so do.

In 1960 the farmers of the diocese of Edmundston were having financial trouble; their Madawaska Farmers Association was on the verge of bankruptcy. Their manager had been spending more than he could collect. He left. The Farmers Union asked the bishop to allow me to replace him. My bishop, with my full endorsement, whether he needed it or not, asked that I get involved with the local Union.

I was young, only 26, enthusiastic and loved challenges and felt helping the union was similar to helping families struggle through hard times. I felt I was helping my neighbor, but Claude Levesque did not see it that way. At a meeting for diocesan priests he sarcastically said, "Priests should help people, not take care of cows and sheep." Everyone knew he was referring to my part-time job and I retorted, "Helping farmers is helping people and not animals. Their job was to take care of sheep, calves, chickens and mine was in turn to help them." He never verbally attacked me again.

I began spending more of my weekends with this group and was dismayed at how pulp mills, food processors and machinery distributors subjugated these landowners. After two summers at army camp I decided I could better serve the Lord by spending my entire summers assisting the Association. It was an enormous assignment because there were sixteen parishes within the Edmundston diocese, and each parish had an association and each association met monthly.

My first major assignment of the Association was to organize the Madawaska Forest Products Marketing Board wherein I soon became the manager. The Board became the agent combatting the monopolies that were the mills, processors and distributors. Within three years the woodlot farmers were getting twice as much for their pulpwood. On the cash crop side, potato, grain and cereal prices stabilized in favour of the farmers. Parishes throughout the province gained from our experiences and emulated our organization.

There was considerable pressure to organize on a provincial level, but I fought this with gusto fearing an eventual schism between Anglophones and Francophiles. We kept it at a regional group where it stands today.

Times they were a changing.

Canada caught up to the Industrial Revolution by way of The Great Depression and World War II. In the 30's when I was born it took about 90% of the population to feed the country using horse and plow. Parents raised families as they had been raised. Small towns and villages were the societal epicenter to most of the population. Tradition resisted change. Slowly and surely the over-sized and under-populated country of Canada transformed from a rural to an urban culture.

At the end of the 50s most rural schools in New Brunswick were independent entities reporting to the parish who in turn reported to the county and upwards to the Provincial Seven School Regions. From time immemorial to the end of the decade schools were built by the Church, administered by the Church, the curriculum regulated by the Church, and the students taught by nuns and brothers of the Church. This was all to change.

In 1960 the Liberals won the Legislative Assembly under Louis Robichaud, the provinces second Acadian Premier. He introduced the Deutch Commission that enacted a wide range of social reforms encompassing language, health care and public schools. The central government was to take over the province's schools holus-bolus, to be paid by a sales tax. This was a stupendous transformation, a journey into the unknown. We were going from a Christian system to a secular society separating the religious from the civic. The civic would be holding the reins.

In my position as Manager of the Forest Products Marketing Board I had an opportunity to speak with Alexandre Boudreau, Co-Chair of the Commission. I asked him if the commission would accept the presence of chaplains in the school system to assist Catholic students with spiritual guidance. He retorted that both the government and the Church couldn't afford such a luxury. He continued that the answer might be in the study of guidance counseling, school psychology or even teaching whereby one could have a Catholic presence, a professional, without the religious trappings. Sort of like the prêtre-ouvriers, the working priests, in France. And, best of all, on the government's purse

Chapter VIII

AWAKENING

In January 1963 I was in my room fighting a bad flu when the resident nurse gave me a penicillin shot prescribed by the doctor. In about 30 minutes my hands got numb and I had shortness of breath. I was burning up with what I supposed was a high temperature, so I opened the window for fresh air and the door for fear of isolation. A passing priest came in an asked what seemed to be my problem. He called the nurse who upon arrival gave me a shot of epinephrine to counter the anaphylactic shock caused by the penicillin and then called the doctor. The numbness completely enveloped my body and the priest gave me the last rites; the sacraments given to people who are perceived to be near death. I was unconscious for a short time and upon revival I heard the priest commenting that my breathing seemed better. Sensation and warmth slowly returned over 30 minutes and I was then ambulanced to the hospital where I convalesced for a week.

I gradually recuperated but I had wretched health for the next two years. The Dean of Studies gave me a reduced load and I had to resign from all other responsibilities. I missed many classes, sometimes a week at a time, which I felt unfair to the students. I therefore approached the bishop and asked for a two-year sabbatical to enable a full recovery. I mentioned the comments from Alexandre Boudreau about guidance counseling and the prêtre-ouvriers and he thought it a good idea.

I enrolled in the University of Moncton with the intent of cramming as many courses into two years without worrying about grades. After I was refused billeting from several French rectories, I was graciously welcomed by an English parsonage presided over by Rector Father Anthony McDevitt and his assistant Father Peter McKee. For two years I celebrated Mass every third Sunday, occasionally during the week, and I couldn't have asked for better friendship or accommodation. I felt at home for two wonderful years and my English improved considerable under their tutelage.

Psychology was the discipline I undertook. I was the oldest student but both faculty and students treated me with respect and acceptance. I studied clinical psychology and guidance counseling and planned on mastering in clinical psychology but I worried clinical psychology would have a too positive transfer from patients. During therapy sometimes a client will transfer his emotions onto the therapist. In a negative transfer the therapist becomes a punching bag on whom the client transfers all his or her resentment and repressed anger as if the analyst was the source of his or her problems. In a positive transfer the therapist becomes the savior, a source of security. My fear was that a patient, male or female, might fall in love with me. My professor assured me the potential conflict would be no different for a married man so I took his advice and my gut instinct and continued with clinical psychology.

I extended my studies through the summers, wrote the exams, and passed all courses without undue stress. I completely recovered my health and these 24 months were a turning point in my life and ministry; psychology not only enriched my life and ministry but also gave me a better understanding of the gospels.

It wasn't long before my theoretical education was put to practical use.

There was a couple in the parish where I was residing and celebrating Mass whose marital occlusion came to my attention – as both priest and psychologist. They seemed to be a nice couple who always attended Mass with their three children. They appeared to love one another but apparently on the least confrontation he would go berserk and beat her, often severely. This was often triggered by his heavy drinking. The last straw for her was when he beat her so severely she required hospital attention; he nearly killed her. She subsequently went to court and received a restraining order against him.

For six months he claimed he stopped drinking and beseeched her, and anyone who would listen – priests, nuns, friends and me – about his sobriety, his contrition and his promise to reform. Father McKee asked if I would see him to ascertain if reconciliation was possible.

In an early session he first said he wasn't drinking and then claimed he wasn't drinking very much. My antennae began to twitch for all concerned felt his drinking was the basic cause of his hostility. When he told me it only took one beer for him to derail, I felt booze was not the problem, but lack of self-control was. He claimed he loved his wife and children and I believed him. When I mentioned his problem wasn't alcohol he laughed demonically and I began to fear sadism, the tendency to derive pleasure, especially sexual gratification, from inflicting pain, suffering, or humiliation on others. When I attempted to further investigate this theory he just walked out. If my diagnosis was right, I felt his wife was in danger. During one of our sessions I asked if I could see his wife; he concurred. She too consented to a meeting with me and in early times she related an incident where her husband forced himself upon her along a railway track. After seven years of marriage and three children she claimed sex always hurt her and she didn't even know what constituted an orgasm. Upon advice from female friends she went to her family doctor whereby he conducted a minor operation, possibly the clearing of clitoral and labial adhesions, and forthwith she began to enjoy sex.

I sensed this was when the real trouble started because when she began enjoying sex her husband developed erectile dysfunction; the inability to achieve and maintain an erection of his penis enough for mutually satisfactory intercourse with his partner. He not only had to drink to be able to function, he felt humiliated by his lack of purpose and his wife's seeming superiority. He also began to hate himself. This self-loathing, humility and inferiority shifted into a hidden hatred for his wife; a transfer of hate from himself to his wife. His meaningful love was now detestation and he acted accordingly. I felt it was a clear case of sadism. I consulted my professor of Psychophysiology who had seen the couple in family counseling, and he admitted he had been hoodwinked by believing alcohol was the basis of the disorder. He strongly recommended I warn the wife because homicide was within the realm of possibilities.

The couple eventually ended up in divorce court and her attorney asked me to attend. I refused on the eventuality the husband might later need my clinical support. The husband blamed everything on her infidelity and there would have to be 30 hours in every day for her to have had so many assignations. The judge said he wasn't inclined toward divorce, so he gave them six months for *his* clinical assistance and assessment; support and evaluation with and by me.

She misunderstood the Judge's decree and arrived at my door. I had to send her away because the judge ordered her husband's consultation, and his alone. He then showed up and over the next ten days we met for three hours every day. On the tenth day he reached an epiphany of sorts, an intuitive leap of understanding. He did admit he hated himself and transferred this hatred upon his wife. After only 25 hours of therapy he had this insight. Insight is the main goal of client-centered therapy. Client-centered therapy is a counseling approach that requires the client to take an active role in his or her treatment with the therapist being nondirective and supportive. It is like being lost while walking in the dark when all of a sudden a light turns on; everything is clear. You can now act because you now know or see where you are going.

He also admitted if his wife hadn't left him he would probably have killed her. He repeatedly stated he loved his wife dearly but when I questioned this ambiguity he answered he hated himself, he wanted to kill himself but didn't have the intestinal fortitude to carry it out so he would kill whoever was closest to him, probably his wife. To me, this answer shed a lot of light on crimes of passion and domestic violence.

I advised the wife and court that she had to stay away from him because he was sadistic, a man who having the tendency to derive pleasure, especially sexual gratification, from inflicting pain, suffering, or humiliation on others.

This marital conflict was just an introduction into the trials and tribulations I would be facing throughout my life as a clinical psychologist and a Roman Catholic priest. I didn't have to wait long.

A woman from Moncton, Pam, was recently arrested and accused of killing her husband. Seven years previously she was arrested for infanticide, the intentional killing of children under the age of 12 months but was acquitted due to lack of evidence. Her lawyer was a member of our parish and approached Father McDevitt for assistance. He said he saved her once, but she was headed for the noose this time around. He couldn't save her life, but we could save her soul. A major barrier, however, was her refusal to see a priest.

I was recruited to approach her as a psychologist and not a priest. Her background was ambiguous. My research indicated she came from a good Christian family, had two boys aged nine and ten, but early in adolescence she became unmanageable. I decided to delve into her teenage years.

I was admitted into her cell; my first visit to a jail. I wore my clerical collar. Movies cannot portray the starkness, the cacophony, the sense of loneliness, desperation, anger and helplessness that pervaded her demeanor. I felt I was in a tiger's cage – alone with a tigress.

She opened our meeting by vehemently saying she didn't want to see a priest. She followed this rancour by asking if I wasn't afraid to be alone with her. "After all, I did kill two people."

I tried to reach her through her boys. Finally, she succumbed and asked a favor. She wanted passes to St. Patrick's Center for her boys. St. Patrick's Center was a recreational center administered by the English Roman Catholic parishes of Moncton. Their swimming pool was a main event. I told her Father McKee had already granted this request and they had already been in the pool and had participated in some sporting events. I added that the Father was keeping an eye on them. Father McKee was dedicated to youth development and was revered by the young. She mellowed and we moved on.

Henceforth we got on amicably; talking intelligently as adults. Her anger dissolved and she appeared comfortable with my presence and my questions. We started by discussing her youth and I was shocked to hear she had been molested when she was but twelve years old. I was further dismayed when she told me the molester was a priest who, for obvious reasons, became a close friend of the family. Her mother upon hearing the account, instead of conveying love, support and understanding slapped her face. She screamed she was evil and was going to hell.

Pam became uncontrollable; traumatized by both the molestation and her mother's rejection. Her mother told her she was evil, so she was going to prove her right. Hormone secretion added to her confusion. This was the time of life when she needed love and support and not rejection. She felt guilty where blame was requisite. She felt dirty when she needed cleansing. She felt sinful when atonement was required. She needed support and protection and the priest who was supposed to be her "good shepherd" turned out to be a wolf in shepherd's clothing. Her mother refused to believe the wolf was devouring her daughter.

She was full of pain and fear and her self-image and self-confidence were destroyed. Her fear and pain transmuted into anger; anger being a survival emotion to protect her from the fear and from danger. Anger became an essential part of her life. Alcohol, drugs and sexual promiscuity became a form of self-destruction, punishing herself for her supposed sinfulness. The damaging behavior was also a form of pain killer. She was on an emotional roller coaster.

Our conversation continued with her telling of her marriage when she was eighteen years old and the subsequent birth of three children. One day, under the influence of either alcohol or opiate, in an outburst of anger, she suffocated her third child, an infant girl. I felt she unconsciously killed her child thereby preventing her from going through all the pain she herself had suffered.

She was immediately arrested and sent to a psychiatric ward for assessment. Included in the theoretical support was spiritual sustenance from a Roman Catholic priest. When the Chaplain entered the room, she threw a tantrum. The rage was so intense all in attendance thought she was possessed by the devil. She now revealed to me, for the first time to anyone, that the visiting priest was the same cleric that had abused her those 10 years previously.

She went to court but was found innocent due to lack of evidence.

Toward the end of the session she sobbed with great pain; pain from deep within. After 50 years I can still see the pain in her face. *Why do I destroy those I love?* I had just received the answer from the sadist who was on the verge of killing his wife.

After this three hour session I returned to the rectory and talked with Father McDevitt who told me the priest in question was still Chaplain at the hospital and that the administration had been asking Archbishop Norbert Robichaud, first chancellor of the University of Moncton, to replace him but to no avail. The administration apparently asked the Chaplain to stay clear of the maternity ward during nursing time. A request he continued to ignore.

After talking with Fathers McDevitt and McKee I decided to take the bull by the horns and notify the Archbishop. I told him something extremely unpleasant would happen if the Chaplin remained in place and he should prepare himself for the consequence. I continued that any psychologist would testify that the sexual abuse by this priest could explain the detainee's uncontrollable behavior. It could make the difference between murder and manslaughter, the difference between life and death.

Capital punishment was not abolished in Canada until 1976.

The Archbishop thanked me for the information but two days later Father McDevitt told me the Archbishop had called Pam's attorney forbidding him from using the information in court. Both Father McDevitt and I were incensed. Her attorney then contacted the Crown's Attorney and negotiated a deal, "Reduce the accusation from murder first degree to manslaughter and I'll keep the Church out of the trial." It worked as Pam got 15 years in a woman's penitentiary in Ontario.

Apparently, Pam endured incarceration with relative composure. She even took the responsibility for the Chaplin's Alter Guild, the person chosen to prepare for Mass, to prepare for the meeting of the people with God. She served an abbreviated sentence and it is believed she never returned to New Brunswick and lives or lived a modicum of a normal live.

Several months later the bishop, Archbishop Norbert Robichaud, came to preside at a ceremony at our parish, St. Bernard's. When I greeted him, he shocked me by stating, "It is priests like you who are bringing down the Church with your studies in psychology and sociology. You should do like the apostles who left everything to follow Jesus." He caught me off guard, but I replied, "St. Paul continued weaving tents and did not want to be in charge of anyone."

Unperturbed he insisted "You should be 100% dedicated to your priesthood ministry, not to psychology."

I just walked away but have always regretted not replying that the one's bringing down the Church are bishops like him covering up for pedophile priests. In his sermon that day he said the Jews would convert to Christianity and afterwards we would have the end of the world. Unfortunately, he was respected by his clergy.

An interesting sidebar occurred some 50 years later when the then Archbishop of Moncton, Father Valéry Vienneau, invited the victims of pedophilic priests in his archdiocese to report complaints to a retired judge of the Supreme Court of Canada. He avowed the diocese would accept the findings, recommendations and penalties put forth by the judge without going through the ordeals of a civil court. This, I considered, was a true Christian, a good shepherd who protected his sheep from the wolves. What a breath of fresh air!

Considerably more will follow on this issue.

Chapter IX

Two Too Many

In the summer of 1960, before leaving for Camp Petawawa, the Dean of Studies told me to prepare a course of Philosophy for September semester. I asked why he was dismissing Father Jean LaChance, his regular philosophy professor.

Father Jean Guy LaChance was a Eudist and Professor of Philosophy. For a reason unknown to most, he listed his name as Jean Guy Pepin in the telephone directory. I asked the Dean why he was circumventing Father LaChance. He said he wanted to prevent trouble at fall semester because it was rumored LaChance intended on failing some students who had belittled his class "favorite"; apparently, they enjoyed starting rumors and watching his so-called favorite running to report them to LaChance. Father Boivin, Dean of Studies, was aware of the situation and knew trouble was forthcoming and wanted to nip it in the bud. He told me to go to Camp Petawawa, enjoy my summer and not show up until September.

LaChance seemed to be very popular with the students; almost every day one could see a dozen students chatting and joking with him. They seemed to like his classes whereby he weaved sexual connotations into his psych lectures. This was great fun and novel for the neophyte students, yet they weren't naïve enough to miss his obvious sexual inclinations. They laughed behind his back while his superiors took this popularity as an indication of wisdom and teaching skills. The students also enjoyed watching his expression change to one of longing when a favorite joined the group or simply passed by. He owned a car he used for sexual persuasion; either as a loan or for connubial "country rides" or off to soft-porn drive-in movies across the border in Madawaska, ME; movies like Clockwork Orange. It was odd but many priests felt crossing a border gave them liberty; either into the US or even into Québec.

One day in the early 90's I was talking to Leopold Lang, the present Dean of Students; not to be confused with Dean of Studies. Leopold was a good friend; reliable and honest. I looked toward the entrance and saw LaChance once again surrounded by about 20 students.

If memory keeps me company, our conversation went like this:

"How long have you been Dean of Students, Leopold?"

"Almost six years."

"Do you feel you've done a good job?"

"Yes, for the most part."

"Just look at the entrance and tell me again if you've done a good job."

Looking awkwardly, Leopold replied, "I know. I know. We all let this one slip through the cracks."

"You're not the only one, Leopold; too many of us have looked the other way too often with too many of our brethren. We have knowingly allowed priests like LaChance off with impunity. He's dirty and you know it. I know it. The bishop knows it. How many lives does he have to ruin before we do something?"

"Circumvention is much easier than confrontation, Leo."

"Yes, it is, but we're no different than Pontius Pilate washing our hands in the font of academic and religious freedom rather than facing our responsibility. It is easier to verbally condemn them as "sick" or "different" rather than call them what they are, criminal predators. Priests who are pedophiles are wolves among the sheep. We have a bishop doing nothing about the travesty. We have a university administration doing nothing. We are doing nothing, and we have a student body watching LaChance groom his victims like a cat with a mouse while enjoying the demonstration."

As expected, LaChance fought to retain his class and position of Homeroom Professor but the Dean held his ground. LaChance was left to augment my class by teaching an hour a week on Bible Introduction. When I finished preparing the September report cards, I noticed more than half of the students had failed LaChance's sole course. They had good grades in all subjects but his and it questioned whether the students were boycotting Father LaChance or Father LaChance was getting even with the students; perhaps a touch of both.

I reported the incident to the Dean of Studies who was not the least surprised and assured the students something was amiss and would closely monitor and correct the situation. Father LaChance took the offensive telling the Dean and other members of the faculty the students were ganging up against him. The Dean came to me with the dilemma and when I told him about LaChance's favorites his response was simply, "Don't tell me he's one of those." He immediately confronted LaChance and the rest of the year went smoothly enough but my relations with LaChance were frigid and ever remained thus.

In 1977 there was an opening for a professor of psychology; I applied but was rejected. The Dean of Studies was now Father LaChance – Father Luck in translation. The name certainly fit because he lived a charmed life.

He wrote an agreeable enough letter with his regrets stating the school really needed an Experimental Psychologist and I was a Clinical Psychologist. The individual they accepted was anything but an Experimental Psychologist being a Freudian Psychologist. Nonetheless, it was clear Father LaChance didn't want me on his staff.

His denying me of the psych position created a difficult relationship between the two of us for decades to come. I didn't have any input into his early replacement by the Dean of Studies, but he didn't take it that way. He was a pain in my Royal Canadian Derrière.

In 1978 there was an opening for a Professor of Philosophy; this time around, however, I lobbied the Students Council and the Professors Association. I acquired the position, but I was still working under LaChance. Our relationship was polite but distant and I had consolation knowing his term as Dean of Studies would expire in a year as they were appointed for three-year terms.

In my opinion Father LaChance was far too selective in his teachings of Sigmund Freud. In freshman classes he postulated on the existence of the libido, eroticism, and completely ignored repressed memory of early childhood abuse and molestation. This was obviously, at least to me, a discriminatory practice to elide over his deviant behavior. I saw it, the students saw it, but the church hierarchy didn't see it or preferred not to see it and to disregard the obvious. A practice too often repeated.

In 1986 Bishop Gerard Dionne replaced Bishop Lacroix who retired due to ill health and positioned my fellow Diocesan, Father Robert Simard, to open *L'Ecole de la Foi* – the School of Faith. The School of Faith at that time addressed adults of all ages, married or single, who desired to learn more about their faith and to be active witnesses to the teaching of Jesus and his apostles in their parish. Simard was the charter director.

L'Ecole de la Foi was a challenge but Robert was well respected by the students and his staff and up to the task. The association consisted of weekend sessions for lay Catholics who would arrive at the Diocesan Centre on Friday evening for night devotions. Lectures would continue through Saturday and would end with Sunday Mass. It was a huge success.

After his term as Dean of Studies, LaChance spent more time at the diocesan office promoting his opportunity to become Director of *l'Ecole de la Foi*. Since two priests of the Eudist Order had become Bishop of

Edmundston Diocese, the appointment to Director of l'Ecole de la Foie could be a good steppingstone to further promotion. He succeeded in making the first step.

He replaced Father Simard who had to resign due to ill health. A few months later LaChance told Simard he was unwelcome at the school. Father Simard was understandably hurt and with good reason as he started the school and built it to its present success. He was now ostracized and ousted by the nefarious LaChance.

In December 1987 he ousted me as well. I understood my dismissal but not Simard's – not until he related another story about LaChance.

Father LaChance's preferred student of 1960 remained his favorite. The young man graduated with a BA, became a schoolteacher; married, and had a son. The relationship between man and boy, however, never changed. The two bought a duplex together with an adjoining door.

Simard had an occasion to visit LaChance when his favorite's son was 13. LaChance was stroking the boy's face remarking to Simard that he liked the feel as the young man was just starting to grow facial hair. The boy seemed uncomfortable, so Simard told LaChance the act was both inappropriate and unacceptable. Simard and LaChance were never friends but after this incident LaChance forthwith treated Simard as an enemy.

At 15 the favorite's son died in a skiing accident. The calamity was under suspect because he was deemed by his peers to be an excellent skier and his tracks went from top of the slope directly into a tree at the bottom. Although it was never brought to an inquest, rumors abounded as to whether it was an accident or suicide; suicide because of childhood molestation. LaChance harped upon the death in class for months after the tragedy feeding fuel to the fire as to whether he was suffering pain or guilt.

LaChance hoped to be appointed Rector of the Parish of St. Andre when he retired but was rejected by the parishioners. The congregate had been traumatized by a priest by the name of Rino Deschenes, a convicted pedophile, and were overly wary of new appointments. Whenever LaChance's name was put forward as a new rector a mother, whose son and daughter had LaChance as a professor, stood before the commune and said, "We don't need another General Boucher in St. Andre." LaChance felt the heat and left for Quebec City.

One of the most telling stories related to me was about a student who had the "privilege" of driving in LaChance's car; apparently for being student of the year. He was so proud of the honor he didn't realize LaChance was simply grooming him as a lover. The day LaChance decided to make his move he had him drive the car to an outdoor movie theatre. The student was somewhat shocked to have a priest taking him to see a drive-in movie, but he understood soon enough when LaChance grabbed his crotch. He panicked, started the car and drove away in such a hurry he pulled the speaker off the post and broke the car window. The students had a field day upon hearing the story the following day.

The instances could be considered humorous if it wasn't for the tragic reality of the ones that didn't get away.

In 1985 there were only four priests left on the staff at the university in Edmundston; two Eudist's, including Father LaChance, and two Diocesan priests counting myself. Things they were a-changing because when the university opened there were 15 priests attending to the students.

Chapter X

VATICAN II

The autumn of 1967 was a new beginning for the Church, the world and for me. The Second Vatican Ecumenical Council had closed in 1965 with its resounding changes, the Premier of New Brunswick was implementing the Deutch Commission with monumental alterations to the school system, College St. Louis was to be a lay administered coed University, and I was returning to Edmundston with a Master's degree in Clinical Psychology.

To encapsulate, Vatican II renewed consecrated life (the public profession of the evangelical counsels of poverty, chastity and obedience), revised charism (the theological term for the extraordinary graces given to individual Christians for the good of others), the ecumenical (the visible and organic unity of different Christian churches and efforts toward dialogue with other religions), the widespread use of vernacular languages in the Mass instead of Latin, the subtle disuse of ornate clerical regalia, the ability to celebrate the Mass facing the congregation, et al. According to Pope Benedict XVI, the most important and essential message of the council is the Paschal Mystery; the passion, death, resurrection, and glorification of Jesus Christ. Paschal means "passing over" in Greek and the Mystery defines the divine truth and life. The Council confirmed the importance of the liturgy, public worship, whereby Christ redeemed mankind.

Vatican II had a most profound effect on me as well as the Catholic Church in general – drastic, dramatic, but refreshing. A very dogmatic church changed to a more pastoral ministry; from a legalistic approach to an idyllic outlook. The windows and doors were euphemistically opened and fresh air blew over the parishioners. Canada went a step further by allowing priests switch from Roman Catholic to Anglican ministries, and vice versa. Married Anglican priests could move into Catholic rectories with their wife and children but with the caveat that if the wife died the priest could not remarry.

The animosity bestowed upon other religions for centuries, especially Protestants and Jews, was negated. Before the ecumenical, Jews and

Protestants were considered sinful and metaphorically "bad." In my primary school days, without having running water or electricity, we had to tote pails of water to clean the floors. On one occasion I was asked by the teacher whether we had a mop at home. I said we did but it was a Protestant mop. Everyone understood the allegory that the mop was bad, it was worn out.

The clergy and the laity accepted the Vatican II changes with open arms.

In my hiatus away for tutelage, I had witnessed firsthand the disastrous consequences of pedophile priests and the cover-up by an Archbishop. I had been exposed to the Rogerian Client Centered School of Therapy. Person-centered therapy (PCT) is also known as person-centered psychotherapy, person-centered counseling, client-centered therapy and Rogerian psychotherapy. PCT is a form of psychotherapy developed by psychologist Carl Rogers in the 1940s and 1950s. The goal of PCT is to provide clients with an opportunity to realize how their attitudes and behavior are affected. Although this technique has been criticized by behaviorists for lacking structure and by psychoanalysts for providing a conditional relationship, it has proven to be an effective and popular treatment.

Studies in Psychology also gave me a different outlook on life and pastoral work. Carl Rogers' Client Centered Therapy was an eye opener for me as I tended to be far too directive, telling people what to do.

With Carl Rogers I learned I could not change people. People can change themselves and the therapist is a mirror that reflects the feelings of the client without being judgmental. It allows the client to understand him or herself and find their own solutions to their problems; to find their own way. It is a little like the old Chinese proverb, "Give a man a fish and you feed him for a day. Teach a man to fish and you feed him for life." Client Centered approach to counseling has been very effective not only for clinical counseling but for spiritual counseling as well.

Contrary to Archbishop Robichaud, I saw psychology and the Gospel as reinforcing each other and not destroying one another. I was going from teaching mathematics to psychotherapist and teaching psychology. It was a new beginning.

The Deutch Commission was paramount, changing the landscape and my life from a totally secular position to a quasi-secular-lay position. The transition from the Eudist's Fathers to a lay administration went relatively well. As expected, a few priests could not accept the transition and retired. Co-educational status was particularly odious to one professor who predicted the university would become nothing but a whorehouse. Another priest was so depressed he died from a heart attack at the early age of 55. Father Bourque, the University Director, attempted to allay this fear by offering courses to more mature women; versus girls in their teens and early twenties. He mostly enrolled them from office clerk pools in the local paper mills. It worked superbly.

There were now more lay professors than priests and the laymen established an association. Many Eudist's felt threatened by the transition to a lay administration and vulnerable to a professor's association. Since I was a diocesan, a priest within an ecclesiastical district under the jurisdiction of a bishop, and not Eudist I was perceived as a good compromise for both sides and was elected as the first president of the Professors Association. The transition went really well and I actually enjoyed being a liaison between the two supposedly extreme entities. All being Christians, they had more in common than deviance.

Many of the priests were still wearing the soutane or cassock in the classroom but I decided to replace it with a lab coat. I felt clerical garb might deter the students from speaking their mind or asking questions. Additionally, the soutane was a nuisance as the bottom always required cleaning due to dust, mud, snow or slush being absorbed.

I canvassed my students for their opinion regarding priest's attire in class and they opined the clerical collar was admissible, but the soutane belonged only in church – or the Dark Ages. Other priests wanted to follow suit but were apprehensive about the bishop's reaction. I approached the bishop and surprisingly he yielded to the students' opinions. All but two switched to lab coats. Things they were a changing.

As the school system in 1968 was now provincial, I began guidance counseling two afternoons a week in the Grand Falls school district. After one year the School Board offered me a full-time job to organize the Pupil Personnel Services for the district. The intent of the service was to assist students in career counselling using Aptitude and IQ testing as well as career information. It identified the students with special needs such as cognitive, physical, social, or emotional difficulties during their developmental process. It also identified exceptional students who could be shown unique career paths. The provision also provided individual and family counseling.

I gladly accepted the position but had to move to Grand Falls from Edmundston which turned out to be a task more difficult than I anticipated. I ended my tutorial position at the University, but lodging became a problem. I went to three separate parishes before I could find a room. The first two had ample space but rejected me because they considered me more lay than secular; a guidance counselor and not a chaplain. I was rejected by St. George rectory and *L'Assomption* parish but finally accepted by *"Les Freres de l'instruction Chretienne"* (The Brothers of Christian Instruction).

Chapter XI

THREE TOO MANY

Throughout my life I have had ambivalent feelings about Bishop Fernand Lacroix, Archbishop of Edmundston 1970-1983; he was a Eudist and an enigma. I believe he was a very good man, an excellent administrator, but he showed a blind eye toward pedophile priests. Another case in point was Father Deschenes.

Father Rino Deschenes was my junior by about 15 years. He was involved in the student association at college and was highly involved with Boy Scouts of Canada when Father Claude Levesque was diocesan chaplain. We were only on a salutation relationship, but his reputation preceded him. We became long-arm associates when I replaced him as assistant priest at St. Andre in 1969 and he was transferred to the same position at Riviere Verte.

I had been assistant priest at St. Andre in 1965 for one year and I looked forward to my return. While previously there, I organized *La Jeunesse pas Achalie* (the Youth of Achilles). They were a very dynamic group of parishioners between the ages of 15 and 25 who were sort of left behind by society. They were an eclectic group ranging from high school dropouts to premarital adolescents. We began by having study groups and lectures but soon morphed into social gatherings having picnics and dances. In short order they accrued enough money to buy a plot of land where the municipality later built a recreation center.

Upon my return I was surprised Boy Scouts in the parish had been disbanded and the group *La Jeunesse pas Achalie* had folded. The charter members were five years older and had moved on in life. *La Jeunesse pas Achalie* may have served its purpose for them, but where were new members?

I had really enjoyed working with the adolescents of St. Andre but now the youth were aloof. I conveyed my concern to one parent who had five sons, the oldest having "graduated" from *La Jeunesse pas Achalie*. The other four quit Boy Scouts when one related that at camp he was awakened in the middle of the night by Father Deschenes fondling his privates. Their friends quit as well. Adieu to Boy Scouts at St. Andre. I now understood the current reservations of the youth and I saw firsthand how one pedophile priest can cause so much damage to a parish.

During summer vacation he would invite boys to his private camp on Baker Lake near his old diocese. The rector of this bishopric reported to Bishop Lacroix how shocked he and his parishioners were about the happenings at the camp. Nothing was done.

In 1974 parishioners from Riviere Verte complained to the bishop about Father Deschenes' sexual abuse of minors and threatened to take him to court. He was "banished" to Laval University for one year and was then to return. I was on the nominating committee and I refused to participate in his nomination and recommended he be defrocked. Instead he was sent to the diocese of Québec as school chaplain. The effrontery and stupidity! It was like putting a fox in a henhouse.

When Deschenes was removed from Riviere Verte and sent to Laval, many rumors circulated Father Claude Levesque may have been instrumental in initiating Deschenes wayward ways. The probability was possible since Father Levesque was Deschenes parish priest when he was a Boy Scout.

In 1975 I was placed on the Nominating Committee for the positioning of priests in the diocese. In this new honorific position Bishop Lacroix told us Father Deschenes was returning to the diocese after his so-called sabbatical at Laval University. All concerned were well aware his so-called leave of absence was really a cover-up for complaints of sexual abuse to minors. I queried the Bishop as to the wisdom of this move and he told me Monsignor Mathieu Mazerolle, a neophyte psychologist, assured him Deschenes was rehabilitated. I questioned the capability of Monsignor Mazerolle making this assessment and recommended Father Deschenes not return to the diocese unless professional diagnosis allayed my fears. I recommended the priest be expelled from priesthood. He was, nonetheless, appointed as a school Chaplin in Québec. He was not defrocked but just shuttled around; shuttled to a position of authority among children.

To aggravate the situation the Rector of Baker Lake, Father Benoit Bosse, told Bishop Lacroix his parishioners were shocked by Deschenes presence and pleaded for the bishop to do something. Nothing happened except I was removed from the Nominating Committee.

It's easy to criticize but one should not throw stones in glass houses. Although Bishop Lacroix was wanting in his supervision of Father Deschenes, I was in the same diocese yet did nothing to address his horrendous transgressions. I was working in the same diocese as he, I knew him, yet consciously or unconsciously I circumvented the acts of pedophilia being conducted right under my nose.

Some 40 years later, in 2015, Deschenes pleaded guilty to five sex-related charges, including indecency and sodomy and was sentenced to seven and a half years in prison.

One may contemplate how many victims would have been spared had he been defrocked and brought to court in 1975.

Chapter XII

GROUP HOMES

The world was changing in the 1960s as never before; the civil rights movement, female activism, the Chinese Cultural Revolution, the assassinations of John, F. Kennedy, Martin Luther King and Robert F. Kennedy, sexual freedom, TV domination, the ramping-up of the Vietnam War, the Cuban Missile Crisis, and the American Civil Rights Act that politically polarized that country to name but a few. In Canada, the Québec quiet revolution activated francophone nationalism and the Canadian Bill of Rights was instituted. But for me, the clergy, and indeed the world, the largest impact of the 60s was the Second Vatican Council. In Canada, schools, hospitals and colleges went from church to secular and governmental control.

With the advent of socialized medicine, the priest lost his role as the most important professional in the parish. When someone now gets sick, they go directly to the hospital whereas previously they would call the priest. The priest was the adjudicator of life and he would determine the patient's next step, and the responsibility of the patient's family. Increased education within the parish drastically diminished the role of the priest.

My home diocese was rural and comprised of agriculture and forestry. The arrival of tractors meant a farmer could increase his production, but he now needed more land so bought adjoining acreage. My home parish went from over 400 farms in the 1950s to about ten today. Present day farmers are of higher education and consequently do not need assistance in agronomy from the parish priest. Similar advancement occurred in forestry; heavy equipment such as the chainsaw and tree harvester has significantly cut the number of lumbermen.

The social hour after Sunday mass has been replaced by radio, television and the social media. The priest has lost his role as father of the parish; his job as accountant, doctor, lawyer, and agronomist. Professionals have replaced him. The priest is now restricted to spiritual counseling and religious services.

With the exodus of so many priests from their calling and the collapse of seminary recruitment, priests now have their mission concentrated on weekend religious services. In the area of my home parish there are four parishes and one priest which at one time had seven rectors. Present day altar "boys" are grown men. Sunday attendance has dropped drastically. The churches of the four parishes used to be filled every Sunday but today not one church is full.

Things were changing and changing rapidly; changing faster than any time in the two millennia of the Church. We went from full pews to empty or almost empty churches. Perhaps this was the fulfillment of an avowal made years past by René Lévesque saying the problem with his province was there were too many steeples and not enough chimneys. (René Lévesque was a reporter, a minister of the government of Québec, the founder of the separatist Party Québécois, and the 23rd Premier of Québec).

Times might have changed but the Church has not kept up to the changing times. Priesthood has lost its attraction for adolescents. The age of horse and buggy is long gone but the Church keeps using the old nag. In my youth the priesthood was very appealing, and parents were honored to have a priest in the family. This is not the case today. Priests today are even embarrassed to wear the Roman collar when they travel.

With the changing times it was fortuitous I became a certified psychologist. I felt I was as much a shepherd in counseling as I was as a priest.

In 1968 I began celebrating Mass every Sunday at a Catholic orphanage in Edmundston. Here I discovered the girls were banished when they reached the physical, but not mental, maturity of fourteen. I was devastated by this action and queried the Mother Superior as to the reason. Her response troubled me further. Apparently, the edict at this orphanage was enacted in fear of the girls becoming pregnant. She didn't respond to my query as to how a girl could become pregnant with only nuns and priests in attendance. She further astonished me with the admission girls could be later readmitted to the facilities if they became pregnant on the outside.

I decided then and there to open a home for rejected teenagers. Our first resident was a 14-year-old expectant mother.

Our Group Home opened in June of 1970 and was the first in New Brunswick. A second opened a few months later in southern NB and was occupied straightaway. Within a year the outcome was so positive the Department of Social Services started opening collective homes throughout the Province; there are 147 today.

Dr. Joseph Cyr, practicing medicine in Grand Falls, owned a small farm he kept for raising horses. When he heard of our group home, he gave us access to his "ranch" house and farm and also the use of a small sugar bush to make maple sugar in the spring. It was a wonderful venue and I wanted the facility to enact a family environment as best as possible. It was to be coed and I wanted the boys and girls to live like brothers and sisters. I also wanted a mother figure in presence.

One of the surprising occurrences the first summer we were together was to discover what terrific therapists' horses made. During these warm months the children had access to Dr. Cyr's horses, and it was amazing and wonderful to see anger disappear instantly when a child in rage petted a horse.

An interesting departure is the story of Ferdinand Waldo Demara, the Great Imposter, who had spent two years in the 50s with the Brothers of Christian Instruction in northern Maine under the sobriquet Brother John. While there he stole the credentials of Dr. Cyr and masqueraded as Cyr as a trauma surgeon aboard HMCS Cayuga, a Royal Canadian Navy destroyer during the Korean War. The impersonations of this wily American included a civil engineer, a sheriff's deputy, an assistant prison warden, a hospital orderly, a lawyer, an applied psychology doctor, a child care expert, an editor, a cancer researcher, a teacher and, as above, a Benedictine monk. The movie actor Tony Curtis played the part of Demara in the 1961 American comedy-drama *The Great Imposter*

I started using nuns as den mothers, but the Mothers Superior wouldn't allow one nun to be on her own, and they couldn't sleep in the same room. They were full of accolades about the project, apparently reminding them of the mother founder of their order, but that's as far as they went. I also needed a separate room and my fear was an inordinate number of adults would displace too many children. I also worried about rumors regarding a priest with either a woman or being alone with children.

I gave a lecture at the local Richelieu Club (a French-Canadian organization similar to the Rotary, Lions or Elks) whereby I told them I was looking for a nun as a den mother. One member jokingly said I should not hire an attractive nun because it wouldn't look too good. I responded I was only looking for a woman who could tolerate the kids' rebelliousness and still love them.

To further understand my commitment in accepting a 14 year old pregnant girl I told the story of Jesus and the woman of ill repute; I said he was speaking at a good reputable club similar to their own when the lady of note fell at Jesus' feet, washed them with her tears, and dried and perfumed them with her hair. This was probably the first time in her life she felt cared for and not rejected. It touched the majority of the Richelieu's. One even told me this was the best lecture he ever attended at the Club. The positive responses were encouraging.

I explained my project to the parish. I told them about a young girl who at the early age of 14 was about to be evicted from an orphanage because of the archaic and non-Christian dictates of the Mother Superior of this institution of the *Order of Marist*. I also warned them to be prepared to see me driving around with young children as if they were my own; perhaps even with pregnant girls. I also asked for some families to volunteer as godparents. Within a week I had more volunteers than I needed and by the beginning of May the house was full of visiting parishioners and nuns.

I met with the school board to inform them of these new students; students that came from across the province upon referrals from social workers, parish priests and religious orders. It soon spread I was opening a home without fear, a home with love and a home as close to a typical family environment as possible. There were institutions in New Hampshire and Quebec with similar expectations, but they were more like boarding schools than a "family." Few weeks into my program I had to turn away 21 applications.

The community and the local teachers were fully cooperative. They treated the children if they were they own; they went the extra mile.

Bishop Gagnon, the aforementioned forethoughtful and forth rightful Bishop of Edmundston, died in 1969 and Father Rino Albert, the Rector of St. George parish who refused to accept me in his glebe, was appointed interim administrator of the diocese until the arrival of Bishop Fernand Lacroix. I opened my home during this intervening period and never consulted with the administrator. I did tell Bishop Lacroix after his Ordination and he was not overly concerned with my omission with Gagnon and showed real interest in my work.

Bishop Lacroix belonged to the Eudist congregation. He was respected and liked by everyone due to his friendly disposition and kindness. He went from college professor to Grand Seminary professor to Superior of the Halifax Grand Seminary to Provincial Superior for all Eudist priests in Canada that included Canadian Eudist's working in South America. He was the first Canadian to be elected to this position as all others came from France. I had met him years earlier and had great respect for his intelligence, his kindness and his optimistic personality. I was delighted with his recent appointment feeling he would support my project – and he did.

Every time I met Bishop Lacroix he would ask about my children and some he even knew by name. On one occasion a young girl asked him where he came from. When he responded Québec, she called him a fibber because he came from his mother. He liked to repose in my Lazy-Boy chair, smoke a cigar and deliberate on what a lovely, homey setting we had established. I was certainly pleased by his words, but it also described the man.

In the mid-seventies the most recent Rector of St. George Parish was retiring and asked if I would like to replace him. I responded to the positive and he thereby approached the bishop with the same question. The bishop was concerned for the children I had taken under my charge, but I told him I could keep them at the rectory. He liked the idea but feared the parish would not like the scheme and what would I do if they rejected the proposal. I told him where my children were not accepted, I was not accepted.

He liked my response and subsequently assembled with the parish council; a group of seven. After the meeting he told me all seven rejected the proposal with one being particularly vehement by saying the bums should all be sent to reform school and I tend to my ministry. The bishop responded that orphanages and reform schools were not the answer for those children, but my approach was. He then asked each councilman if they would take any of the children and to a man they responded negatively. He was very unhappy and chided them by question, "If you don't want them and Leo can't have them, then who will look after them? If the Church rejects the rejected, who will accept them?"

Coming from a family of fourteen I found being childless the hardest part of celibacy. The group home partially fulfilled the void and need as some of the children looked upon me as a father figure, paternal versus liturgical, and even called my parents grandfather and grandmother.

The group home was a God send for the youth and really touched these hardcore kids. One day one of the toughest asked me if, when married, his children could call me grandfather. They weren't the only ones who had their heartstrings touched.

Realizing I couldn't count on finding a sister for a mother figure, a den mother, I started looking for an alternative and I lucked out with an unlikely candidate – a college student. Nicole came from a dysfunctional family and found living at home too depressing. She didn't have a summertime job so a position with us fit both our needs.

Nicole was in her senior year of a BA curriculum and was expecting to continue toward her B.Ed. She was a little shy, sensitive, but wonderful caring with the children. Due to her own insensitive background she had empathy with them and gave them great support. She loved the job; she lost her depression and the children loved her. She wanted to quit college, but I talked her out of the idea, and she continued her higher education in the fall. She did finish post grad in education, taught, married, gave birth to two and had a fruitful life.

When Nicole left for college, I hired my brother's finance Cecile who also came from a violent home. She was just 18 and really clicked with the adolescents.

Cecile was subjected to a few temper tantrums as were the schoolteachers. My presence was called upon on many occasions. I summoned the help of the other students who were more than willing to help. Grabbing and throwing the hairpiece of the school director during such a tantrum was one of many difficult incidents. Verbal tirades were also part of tantrums.

Winter soon followed the potato harvest and preparation for Christmas began. Cecile got into the spirit and involved the girls in housecleaning, baking cookies, meat pies, and Christmas cake. Each of our children had an adoptive family in the community where they could go on special occasions or during recess from their daily round and common task. The first Christmas I had to stop the community from giving more Christmas gifts because each had received more than a dozen. This would have given them an impractical view of reality.

The boys assisted in felling and decorating the tree. We had a most enjoyable Christmas. We went to midnight mass on Reveillon (Christmas Eve) and afterword returned home to a French-Canadian tradition – Tourtiere. Tourtiere is a double-crusted meat pie with a savory pork, beef and onion filling. Cecile and the girls were especially proud of their creation and it was delicious. Gift distribution and unwrapping followed, and all were ecstatic save for one – our "toupee" girl who tried her best to dampen the spirits of all others.

Bad habits were personified by this girl. Without any musical talent she demanded a guitar. I kept her guitar hidden until the last gift was opened thinking and hoping it would heighten her mood. But I was wrong. She had no sooner opened her gift when she complained it was the most boring Christmas she had ever had. It was a hard blow for Cecile and me. I told her Cecile, all her roommates, the parishioners, and I worked for months to prepare the best Christmas we could. She replied she did understand but a Christmas without a mother and father wasn't a real Christmas. This was pure fantasy because she was abused by her stepfather since she was twelve.

After the gift openings we all went to my parents for another Acadian tradition; chicken stew with homemade dumplings. There were of course additional gifts from my parents.

Another episode tested my sang-froid was again in the form of our guitar-toupee girl. She had been sexually molested by her stepfather at the age of twelve. She became uncontrollable, sexually promiscuous, smoked heavily and sold sex for cigarettes. My mother liked saying, "She may be tough, but has a heart of gold. She calls a spade a spade?" My mother was right. Throughout her childhood she had been rejected by those who were supposed to love and care for her. After a year in our home, however, she felt absolute love for me as a father figure and Cecile as a mother.

Unfortunately for us Cecile was getting married and leaving for good. Our unfortunate waif was so terrified of being hurt and abandoned again, suffering the pain of rejection, she unconsciously tried to take the initiative of the break. She reacted by misbehaving at school and fighting with the other members of our group. When I reprimanded her, she dared me to break my promise and banish her from our home. She insisted. I told her I loved her and would not forsake her. She forbade me to love her. I laughed and told her there was nothing she could do about it. Under persistent attention she finally succumbed to our love and began behaving normally; as normal as a teenager can be. She had a boyfriend, got married and after three children left her abusive husband and moved to Montreal. After thirty years of separation I got an unexpected call from Montreal telling me she was the proud grandmother of five. She called to thank me for all I had done for her so many years in the past realizing full well what we sacrificed on her behalf. She still could not understand how I endured such adversity from all the kids and return only patience and love. I was gratified by her words and was again reminded of the leper parable.

Unfortunately for us, Cecile did marry my brother. Luckily, I was able to get another recent BA student, this time a graduate who had stayed with us for two years until she joined Jean Vanier's mission.

Jean Vanier was the son of Canadian Governor-General Georges Vanier and is a Catholic philosopher, theologian, and humanitarian. He founded the international movement of L'Arche (The Ark) Communities. A program where people with development disabilities, people who would otherwise be shut away in institutions, and their friends who assist them can create homes and share life together.

The British Broadcasting Corporation (BBC) headlined on 20 February, 2020, *Revered Christian leader "guilty of sex abuse."*

> A religious leader who founded a celebrated organization for people with learning difficulties sexually abused six women, an internal report found.

Canadian Jean Vanier founded the global network L'Arche in France in 1964 and died last year aged 90.

None of the women he abused were themselves disabled, the report says.

The investigation into Vanier was commissioned by L'Arche International last year after suspicions were raised.

L'Arche in the UK is thoroughly shocked by this news. Jean Vanier was an admired figure and the findings of this report will cause pain for many, " said L'Arche UK's CEO, Loren Treisman in a statement.

The organization is believed to operate in 35 countries, and runs homes and centres where people with and without disabilities live together.

What does the report say?

Vanier had "manipulative sexual relationships" involving "coercion" with at least six women between 1970 and 2005, according to Canadian newspaper the Globe and mail which has seen the report.

The women included assistants and nuns.

The relationships were "characterized by significant abuses of power, whereby the alleged victims felt deprived of their free will and so the sexual activity was coerced or took place under coercive conditions."

Vanier was enabled and shared sexual partners and "mystical" sexual practices with a disgraced priest Thomas Phillippe, according to the Globe and Mail.

Father Phillippe, who dies in 1993, was Vanier's "spiritual father."

Our children attended public schools and we had an excellent relationship with and cooperation from the teachers as well as the community at large. Our children were an extra burden for the teachers because they were not school orientated and class disruption was less than a rarity. Some took to the new rigors as horse to water and one even obtained two grades in one year.

In October, the schools closed for two weeks for potato harvest. Our group went picking potatoes like all the other children. This was difficult as hard work and discipline were not in their vocabulary. The weekly pay packet was the impetus for their labor whereby they had money for the first time in their lives to buy bubble gum, candy and Coke. After the harvest we had a party to celebrate their efforts at hard labor. It was a wonderful summer, but some unfortunately relapsed into their bad behaviors; bad habits of stealing from wherever and from whomever they could, lying, aggressiveness, and blasphemy; habits typical of delinquents.

During the winter of '71 I received a visit from the local founder of the *Institute Voluntas Dei* (God's Will), an educational and social association aspiring toward free-will and choice. He had closed the Seminary of the Institute at the town of Arthurette some 45 miles south of Grand Falls. The location consisted of 200 acres; half farmland and half woodland. The property encompassed a church for the parish of Arthurette and two other buildings large enough for two groups of five kids. After seeing our facility, he offered me his vacant property and any income from renting the farmland or selling timber would go to us.

I closed the home on Dr. Cyr's farm and rented the habitation and accommodated three groups or families as I called them, comprising 17 teenagers. As soon as news spread about the new facility, demands for lodging sky rocketed. This proved there was a tremendous need for group homes in the province of New Brunswick, and likely throughout Canada – and perhaps the US as well.

Father Leo Gregoire, the parish priest of Arthurette, embraced the project and accepted to start a group from his community. He found a mother figure in the person of Sister Florence Daigle; the nuns were finally yielding to contemporary needs. He filled a house *tout suite*. During the summer I kept busy moving our group to Arthurette, remodeling and opening another home with Father Gregoire. Gregoire was short of stature, good humored, loved classical music and had great empathy with everyone. He was an all-around priest.

In 1974 we had two nuns as group mothers, indicative of the major changes in our society. It was quite an expansive experience for them. They were depressed with their present place in limbo and were delighted with this new calling of working with teenagers. It was a gratifying experience for them even if the children were seldom grateful. Most of our kids had very bad family experiences. Every time they allowed themselves to love someone they had been rejected. They had never experienced unconditional love so when thus confronted they had to test this new and alien condition. They generally took the initiative of separation because it hurts less to reject the person you love rather than the opposite. Oh my, but, how they can test you.

If one worked with those kids for the gratitude they would return, one had better get another job. This recalls Jesus's parable of the ten lepers he healed and only one thanked him, the others taking his cure for granted. It can often be very easy to cry out eagerly to God when we are in need, but we should always remember to show our gratitude to God as well as others in our lives for every kindness shown to us.

Our children, being just children, took their healing for granted. Most parents probably lived through the same experience with their children. Mathew 25:40 reads, "Truly I tell you, whatever you did for one of the least of these brothers and sisters of mine, you did for me." St Vincent de Paul told his disciples, "To serve the poor is to serve Jesus." The simplicity of being Christian should mean you help not for gratitude but to see the least of Jesus' children and do to them what you would do to Jesus.

In the fall of 1971, my uncle Father Levite Theriault came back from missionary in India. He belonged to the Holy Cross Order. He was 40 years old and spent 14 years as a missionary in the hills of India and Pakistan and was considered by his Order as one of their best missionaries. Coming home was a cultural shock as the Church in Canada changed so drastically in his absence. He was also struggling with celibacy. I offered him an opportunity to supervise a third group home and he gladly accepted. He was also appointed Chaplain of Thomas-Albert High School in Grand Falls. As nuns were beginning to get interested in our project, he easily found a mother figure. He started our third group with a nun and soon he had a full house; by Christmas of '71 we had a total of 17 children.

After two years Levite left his order and got married and went into social work. I accepted his children. Through political contacts I was able to get him a job as a parole officer and this was his career for the working days of his life. As mentioned, priests before my time had extensive education but no degrees. When they left the priesthood, they were bereft of proper paper and could only get menial occupation. The Provence of Québec realizing the number of gifted priests leaving the priesthood finally gave them equivalency degrees.

From the get-go I promised the children I would never kick them out of quarters; a major commitment they tested time and again. It was like walking a tightrope because I had to retain control while giving them wiggle room. A test trying my patience and trustworthiness happened in February when Father Gregoire was out and his den Sister was supervising. One of the children came running to my group and told me one of the girls was threatening the Sister. Upon arrival I discovered the culprit's only weapon was her mouth. She was a big girl for 16 weighing about 160 lbs. and it took all my strength to restrain her. I grabbed her arms to confine her and shortly thereafter she calmed down, apologized to the Sister and things got back to relative normality. The next day she had blue marks on her arms and shoulders from my grasps.

She had been referred to Father Gregoire's group as being a pathological liar, immature and impulsive.

The following day she went to a neighbor and displayed her bruises. They called her mother who lived a four-hour drive away and the next morning, 20 below zero, we were leaving for school at 7:30 when we were stopped by a car in the driveway. It was our delinquent girl's mother with the leader of the Parti Acadian (a political party in the 70s and 80s that touted the imbalance of services to French Canadiens in New Brunswick) who told me they came to shut down our homes because of me physically abusing children. I continued to school and left them to deal with Father Gregoire. When I returned that evening the ladies were gone but our teenage problem was still there. The incident was reported to the government and Social Services investigated the episode and I and the home were exonerated. That was the end of it. We did not kick her out and three months later our problem child thanked me for having restrained her. She seemed to be a changed girl and was never a problem thereafter.

Another of our assemblage was a 17-year-old girl who was bright, doing well at school but a month before graduation she ran away with another classmate, a girl. I felt I had failed her. About five years later, however, I met her sister by happenstance who informed me our runner was doing just fine. She was married with two children and was a legal secretary. She lived only five miles from my office, so I called her and was invited over for a cup of tea.

She confided how nervous she was while waiting for my visit. She continued by saying her sojourn with us saved her life, but she was ashamed to admit it. She felt guilty for having to live in a group home as if it were a reform school. I confided that I too felt guilty; but guilty for failing her. Our confessionals did us both good and we took a pact that the past was just that and we should be proud what was accomplished and to go on from there.

I still held my regular job with Pupil Personnel Services during the day and I worked with the group home at night. Even though fifty percent of expenses were covered by the province I still struggled to make ends meet. All my scant salary went into the homes. In 1973 the treasurer for the Institution had been collecting the rent of the farm and income from the woodlot contrary to our agreement. I was supposed to get the entire income from renting the farm but the congregation of *Voluntas Dei* reneged on their commitment and took the entire revenue.

The homes were becoming a financial burden for us. Also, Father Gregoire and his Sister den-mother were not too comfortable with these hardcore adolescents following our episode with Social Services. Father

Gregoire, Father Levite and I therefore decided to separate our concerns. Father Gregoire being a member of the Institute and rector of the parish of Arthurette would take over the property and switch it to a home for mentally handicapped. I bought an old six-bedroom farmhouse on 56 acres of land that had been foreclosed by the bank and my uncle, Father Levite, moved there while I moved back to Dr. Cyr's farmhouse.

In 1971 when Cecile got married, I hired May, one of my sister's classmates from college. She just graduated with a B.A. degree and was interested in doing social work. My program was a challenge for her and was like an internship for further education. She worked with me for two years before deciding to commence graduate studies. Back to square-one.

In January of '72 a man approached me with a singular problem. His unmarried stepdaughter was pregnant and refused to consider adoption. This was Cheryl's second child and the first was given up for adoption. He wanted me to convince her that adoption was the correct approach to take. When we met, she seemed highly traumatized about the past adoption and I feared if she allowed the new baby to go, she would only get pregnant again – or worse. She wanted a child for herself. I re-laid this prognosis to her stepfather and he then asked if I would take her into our group home. He offered to pay her board, but I knew that wasn't in the cards. I took her in, nonetheless.

On April 26th she gave birth to a healthy boy. I approached the baby's father the next morning at school and he showed little or no interest in the girl, the event or the baby. Cheryl decided to quit school to attend to her baby; she called him Leo Arthur. She helped May with house chores and filled in for the nuns when they needed a break or when other duties called.

The arrival of the baby changed the dynamics of the home as he was definitely the center of attention. On one beautiful Saturday when he was two or three months old, I asked May to take the kids to the movies in Grand Falls. I had had a tough week and I needed a break from the noise and rigor of the teenagers. The owners of the movie theatre let the group home gang free admission whenever requested. May, Cheryl, the teenagers and I certainly appreciated their generosity. When I asked May to dredge up the old van, she asked what about Cheryl and the baby. I told her to take Cheryl and I would babysit. I added in front of the group I would enjoy babysitting because babies can be loved and they can't hurt you. They got the message.

After they left, I attacked our budget. I was running about $50.00 short for the coming week; nothing alarming, but a deficit nonetheless. I had just finished my paperwork and was changing the baby's diaper when the doorbell rang. It was three nuns visiting from Grand Falls and they certainly had a good laugh seeing a priest change a diaper. Upon leaving, Mother Superior gave me a cheque for $100.00. I didn't know whether to laugh or cry. She blushed fearing she had not given enough. I told her how her windfall saved our bacon and I was now running a surplus. To this day I believe their visit was more than a coincidence.

The first Saturday of October was a beautiful day; the forests were in full fall color; it was sunny and warm. It was a perfect autumn day. I took the group on a picnic to a nearby swimming hole. While the others were playing in the water, I took Leo, now about 16 months, on my shoulders for an uphill hike. We sat in the grass for Leo to romp and I to get a rest when something unforeseen happened. Leo started picking up and marveling at some leaves. He gurgled with pleasure at the beauty of nature. It took a 16-month-old child to remind me of God's wonderful creation. I was now seeing and hearing these wonders through the eyes and ears of a child and I felt overwhelmed.

The kids called me Pere Leo, Father Leo, but when Leo Jr. started talking the best he could do was Polo. This stuck and soon all were calling me Polo. Baby Leo changed the dynamics of the home as he mellowed the harshness of the tough kids. They were able to let their guard down without appearing to be soft. I nonetheless kept a sharp eye and ear open to assure they didn't teach him any bad habits or language.

In 1972 I met with the Director of Juvenile Correctional Services of New Brunswick and we reached an agreement for our home to be considered a half-way house in conjunction with the Kingsclear Reform School, a youth detention center located just 10 km west of the capital Fredericton. The agreement should have worked well and would have if given a chance. It would have been instant conditioning and feedback. The adage "you scratch my back and I'll scratch yours" could be morphed into "you break the law you go to reform school; you behave you are accepted at home."

When an adolescent was put on probation and sentenced to the Reform School, he could also serve his sentence in our home as long as he behaved. If he misbehaved his Probation Officer would send him back to the Reform School. The freedom of our home was a reward for good behavior. The Director of Juvenile Correctional Services told me and the Superintendent of Kingsclear Reform School to repeat the process a hundred times if necessary if it would save a kid. It sounded like a promising program.

We started with a 14-year-old boy but unfortunately after two months he broke into a summer camp along the Tobique River. I called his Probation Officer to take him back to the Reform School. The PB called the Superintendent who went to court and asked the judge to terminate the boy's parole thereby requiring another court order to take him back. I reported the incident to the Director of Juvenile Correctional Services, but he didn't live up to his "hundred times" avowal. He didn't stand up to the Superintendent and enforce his statement – or our agreement. He might have believed in our plan but didn't have the temerity to live up to and apply it. The "status quo" withheld over great potential.

The Kingsclear Reform School is the self-same institution one Karl Richard Toft, a reformatory guard, was convicted of sex offences in 1992. He was reputed to have committed an estimated 200 sexual assaults, was convicted of 34 and sentenced to 13 years in prison. He was regarded as one of Canada's worst sex offenders; worst so caught.

With the potential of alleviating overcrowded reform schools and giving teenage offenders a better chance in life, I was not ahead of my time; I was answering a need of our time.

We were running in so much red ink I had to move two groups to Grand Falls into two farmhouses; we reopened the Dr. Cyr facility again and as mentioned I purchased a 50 acre farm that was in foreclosure. In 1975 I had to close the one remaining group headed by another priest who left the Church and moved them to Grand Falls. I promised all the children when they entered my group home that we would never abandon them. In 1978 I stopped accepting any more children and in 1981 the last one became of age to leave.

The homes had now been running for ten years and I felt I had to move on as well.

Most, with my delight, went to their family homes because either the home environment improved and/or they had changed so drastically their parents could handle them. Others found work while still others got married. In 1981 the last one left. That was the end of my group homes. Social Services of New Brunswick were now organizing group homes.

All and all I was gratified by what I had accomplished. I reminded myself, however, when one works in a profession of assistance you do it for your belief and not for gratitude. On my own initiative, realizing a tremendous need, I opened the first group home in New Brunswick and, as previously mentioned, there are 147 today. Among the total, there are 32 in St. John, 27 in Fredericton, 25 in Moncton, 6 in Edmundston, and

71

5 in Mariachi. Group homes, residential care and supporting housing are under Provincial Residential Services. They publicize group homes as a single-family dwelling for special populations needing a supervised living environment; examples include children and youth in care, individuals with developmental or physical disabilities, individuals recovering from substance abuse, teenage mothers, or victims of domestic violence. Today supervisory incomes range from $30k to $110k Canadian Dollars. I think back when I was worried about a weekly debit of fifty bucks. *Wow!*

Chapter XIII

FOUR TOO MANY

Father Claude Levesque was older than me. He was assistant priest at the cathedral for many years and was very involved with youth education, sports as well as academe. He was very involved with the scout program and for many years was the diocesan chaplain of Boy Scouts. He initiated and was deeply involved with the construction and administration of the parish Recreation Centre. He was also an entertainer; he always had a ready joke. He could tell the same joke five times and it would still be funny. Unfortunately, he could also be sarcastic! Even with the bishop. His tongue was sharp as a sword and a couple of words could slice and dice you.

In 1975 I was on the nomination committee and Claude called me before the meeting and asked me to stop at his office in Grand Falls after the meeting. He wanted to know about all the nominations and I told him about my refusal to participate in the nomination of Father Rino Deschenes. I also mentioned that pedophiles are very hard to treat and the rate of relapse is very high. He listened to me with a poker face. I did not know at the time he was a pedophile, sexually molesting altar boys. I never detected any body language that would indicate he was uncomfortable with the discussion.

Gerard Dionne was bishop of Sault Sainte-Marie, Ontario. He grew up in Edmundston and was about the same age as father Levesque and knew him well. Several years after my discussion with Claude, Bishop Dionne told me Claude was accused of sexually abusing altar boys adding he was a sick man and would be for the rest of his life. He knew about Claude Levesque molesting boys and did nothing about it but in 1987 he expelled me from the ministry and of *L'Ecole de la Foi* because I was getting married. I confronted the bishop about the dichotomy of issues, but he ignored me. Apparently, marriage was a greater sin than pedophilia. Loyalty to the Church is more important than loyalty to Jesus?

Pedophiles are experts in their field. They can detect the victim who will not talk and know how to circumvent rumors and avoid accusations. A congregation of 100 or more will probably contain more than one sexual deviant and possibily one or more victims.

These vignettes reveal how a crafty, intelligent yet malicious person can dupe not only the hoi polloi but the noblesse as well.

Chapter XIV

FORD FOUNDATION FELLOW

In 1972, while I was 38 and still running the homes for excluded teenagers in the Grand Falls School District, the Director of Pupil Personnel Services at the Provincial Department of Education recommended I apply for a Ford Foundation Fellowship. The Ford Foundation, created in 1936 by Edsel and Henry Ford, is a New York headquartered, globally oriented private foundation with the mission of advancing human welfare.

The grant I applied for was an offering to young leaders in poor or rural areas that could be free for one year to do research into alternative or improved methods of orphanage and reform school methodologies. My goal was to visit the kibbutz in Israel.

A kibbutz is a collective community traditionally based on agriculture. It is a planned residential community designed to have a high degree of social cohesion and teamwork. The members typically have a common social, political, religious, or spiritual vision and often follow an alternative lifestyle.

I felt the system could well lend itself to the adolescent needs of Canada, especially rural teens, and said so in my mission statement to the Ford Foundation.

I had read *The Children of the Dream* by Bruno Bettelheim dealing with the raising of children in the kibbutz. The kibbutz seemed to be such a good alternate to our orphanage and our reform schools. Bruno was an Austrian-born psychoanalyst generally in the Freudian tradition. A survivor of both Dachau and Buchenwald he immigrated to the United States and spent most of his career as a professor of psychology at the University of Chicago. He was internationally respected for his work with emotionally disturbed children.

I so applied and surprisingly and gratefully accepted the accolade for I was accepted and received a one-year salary plus the equivalent of a year salary for travel expenses. Regrettably my trip to Israel was cancelled due to Middle Eastern tension so I switched to Plan B which was to visit group homes and reform schools in Canada and the United States.

The closest I could get to the kibbutz practice was to visit Bruno Bettelheim at the University of Chicago where he was Director of the Orthogenetic School for disturbed children. (Orthogenesis is the biological hypothesis that organisms have an innate tendency to evolve in a definite direction towards some goal due to some internal mechanism or driving force.) This was to be one of the highlights of my life. His camp internments gave him an extraordinary insight into the insurmountable human survival instinct. I was accepted for a three day visit at the school and a private interview with Bruno. The school contained 20 residential autistic children; the oldest was 20 and was attending courses at the university. It was my first contact with autistic children.

I attended a case study he led with six social workers and students. He was a very strict disciplinarian and strident in his approach. The case was about an autistic boy who had gone home for the weekend, didn't want to return but was forced back by his parents. Bruno grilled the social worker as to the whys of the situation and upon her negative responses he became very belligerent with little sympathy for her. Her tears did nothing to appease his aggression as he seemed totally concerned for the wellbeing of the child. He was interested in lessons learned and what could have been done to improve the situation as well as what could be done in the future to countermand such events.

I was more or less given full access of the school and I had the promised private interview with Bruno. He was most cordial after I explained my work with adolescents in Canada, my admiration of his book, my interest in the kibbutz, and my desire to improve Canadian group homes through advanced knowledge of foreign successes.

The lesson I learned during my hiatus in Chicago could be summarized as a reinforcement of the client-centered approach; a technique whereby the client is accepted in all their natural complexity and not where the practitioner feels the patient should be in the future. I felt Bruno Bettelheim's approach with autistic children could be used with other teenagers in distress.

After Chicago I headed east to Village Haven in Greenwich Village, New York. Village Haven was a long-term treatment center for female prostitutes and drug addicts started by a catholic priest. In the sixties they were treating opioid addiction with methadone but with limited success. Churches and social services felt this was solely an addiction transfer. They felt psychological counseling and religion could combat drug addiction.

The program included group counseling, individual counseling, arts and crafts, class upgrading, clerical courses, and work programs. The work programs were mainly small "cottage industry" contracts like assembling toys, ballpoint pens and other small contribution projects. The workers were paid by the hour plus room and board. The aim was to imbue self-worth and self-reliance but the success with prostitutes was minimal, at best. The girls found the work tedious and penurious; they were making far above the minimum wage while practicing their "trade" and did not consider prostitution a sin but a career. They are pragmatic living one day at a time, taking a practical approach to problems and affairs. Not being ideologues, they cannot be motivated by Christian doctrines.

As with Bettelheim's autistic patients, I felt pragmatists should be taken at face value, taken as they come in all their natural complexity, and not preached upon. This approach can also be used with teenagers in anguish.

I next visited Vermont social services whereby they were conducting workshops on juvenile concerns. Vermont at the time was attempting to promote group homes as an alternative to orphanages and reform schools. The major difficulty they were encountering was getting and retaining custodians with empathy and patience with teenagers. Guardian turnover was excessive; averaging three couples every two years.

One of the workshop leaders was the director of a group home in Nashville, Tennessee. I was so taken by his presentation I asked to visit his institution. It was sponsored by the Anglican Church. Considerable thought went into developing the establishment. The structure itself was shaped like an "H," like my early school accommodations. Each of the four wings lodged a group of eight; either boys or girls, but not cohabited. Each group had three rooms double occupancy and two single rooms as an award for good behavior and leadership. Each section had its own living room with TV and games table. Sofas and chairs were assembled for lounging and counsel sessions. The cross of the "H" harbored the cafeteria, the laundry and more games. The grounds accommodated small farm animals and a large vegetable garden.

All the teenagers appeared very cheerful and the director attributed their sunny demeanor to the guidance of their wonderful caretakers who made them feel wanted, useful and unthreatened. As discussed in Vermont, good staffing meant everything. The grounds also attributed to the wellbeing of the commune; relative privacy, education, entertainment, and labor. As previously prophesized, an idle mind is the devil's workshop.

When my year was up I felt I had gained superb information to take back to Canada. Just a few items summarized without any order of significance:

1. *Orthogenesis*; the biological hypothesis that the evolution of species is linear and driven by internal factors rather than by natural selection. This theory is largely discredited today.

2. *Lessons Learned*; information should form part of project or program documentation.

3. *Client Centered Approach*; person-centered therapy uses a non-authoritative approach that allows clients more of a lead in discussions so that, in the process, they will discover their own solutions. The therapist acts as a compassionate facilitator encouraging, supporting and guiding the client toward self-discovery.

4. *Pragmatic Approach*; a methodology that assesses the truth of meaning of theories or beliefs in terms of the success of their practical application – using the method which appears best suited to the research problem.

5. *Guardians*; Realizing the importance of good, reliable and committed custodians.

Chapter XV

THE HYPOCRISY OF IT ALL

In 1981 the group home closed but I remained in the farmhouse with Patricia and Leo Junior until 1987. With Pat moving to Ontario and Leo staying with me I again needed a housekeeper and a mother figure to help me raise Leo. I was referred to Rina Bourgoin, a seven-year widow. She was unknown to me but her late husband was my second cousin. She needed work and accepted the position.

In April of that year I started dating Rina and shortly thereafter we fell in love; not love at first sight, but gradual and holding. She was a beautiful woman and I was proud as well as content to be with her and seen with her. There were obvious mixed emotions among the parishioners but I either didn't notice or didn't care.

My work, my career, at this juncture of my life had kept me fully active and satisfied but I now seemed unfulfilled. I was also dismayed; nay disgusted, with the way the Church was heading, especially regarding unrepented, unsanctioned and unpunished priests for their obvious iniquities.

Rina was shocked when I asked her to move in with me. It had never occurred to her I was willing to forgo the priesthood for her love. Her son was positive about the experiment, her daughter less so. Rina accepted my proposal and moved into our group home. After only a few months we decided to get married the following year. It is difficult to imagine, but twenty-nine years after my ordination as a priest, at fifty-three, I felt the need for companionship of the opposite sex.

I told Bishop Dionne our decision to marry and he warned me dispensation might not conveniently arrive from Rome. I told him pro or con we were going to get married. I continued that I couldn't live the life of a fraud as did so many priests by having a "housekeeper" in the rectory. I expounded upon the immunity of sex offenders and the liberalization of the clergy. I related my fear that if present events continued, fifteen years down the road the diocese would be in an unrecoverable mess. My pointless but obvious conclusion was I needed a companion for life and couldn't continue the life of a celibate.

We realized our marriage was not going to be a primrose lane to marital bliss and the trek would be most difficult. We were most anxious about the church because we were obviously devoted Christians and Catholics. We worried about our families. We unnecessarily fretted about Rena's present mother-in-law who comfortably told us I was the only man capable of replacing her son but she was going to miss my sermons in Drummond. Expecting the opposite, we were joyfully surprised how well the old generation accepted our proposed marriage. Our direct families accepted it well, even if my father had hopes of me becoming a bishop.

The Vatican had other feelings. They had strict rules regarding a priest contemplating marriage and they weren't flexible or amicable. Wedding festivities were not allowed. The blessing of the marriage had to be private – bride, groom, two witnesses and the celebrating priest. Involvement in church ceremonies such as reading, preaching or serving at the altar had to cease forthwith, regardless of whether lay people were so sanctioned. I was "defrocked" but not excommunicated. A married Anglican priest can become a Roman Catholic priest and have their wife and children live in the rectory but a Roman Catholic priest that takes the vows of the Church and subsequently marries can never return to the ministry. A misbegotten priest is considered less than a layman in the Roman Catholic Church. Sit in the pews and shut up because you are only tolerated. Oh, the injustice of it all!

It is most difficult to recount my feelings at the time. I was torn between my love of and dedication to the Church and my love of a woman. I was undecided until I made my final decision and then I was enveloped in a state of serenity. I believe it was similar to the event well known to Alcoholic Anonymous attendees, a dry drunk. They explain this as a period when an alcoholic is dry but still feels he can still drink. Everyone resists change and I was celibate from birth and parishioners are instilled with the catechism adage "is, was and ever will be." Nonetheless, most of my colleagues and congregation thankfully understood my dilemma, position and decision.

The law of celibacy for priests was passed in 305 AD at the Synod of Elvira. It was not, however, adhered to until the Second Lateran Council in 1139. In this interim of eight hundred years 39 popes were married and many others had concubines. Many had children as late as Pope Alexander VI (1492-1503) who begat children out of wedlock. The Church has had more years with married clergy than with celibate clergy. The hypocrisy of it all!

The Merriam-Webster Collegiate Dictionary defines celibacy as abstinence from marriage and sexual relations whereas the Church interprets celibacy as only abstaining from marriage. Priests can have sex outside marriage while preaching from the pulpit but it is a sin for their parishioners to have extramarital sex. The hypocrisy of it all!

We experienced similar dichotomy when Vatican II changed the mass from Latin to the vernacular. Many priests and lay Catholics kept to the Latin Mass because it was thought to be the Mass since the inception of Christianity. Jesus celebrated mass in Arabic.

A priest getting married is obviously a major turning point in his life. It is a cataclysmic event as it not only completely changes one's lifestyle but is a schism from tenets believed and honored from childhood. I not only changed my instilled dogma, took a mate but also inherited Rena's three children and a grandchild. Leo Jr. was now fifteen. It was obviously an enormous change in my life. I thought I had a complete life as a priest, but a vacuum was present that marriage satiated. My life was finally to be fulfilled.

In October, six months before our wedding, I asked Father Simard to bless our wedding and he complied. Our problem, however, was not with sanctification but with my dispensation from the Vatican because it would not be forthcoming until April; ergo, no church wedding. Father Simard, however, found a loophole. The loophole is a ritual for an engagement ceremony whereby the couple promise fidelity in a private service and later have the official wedding. Problem solved.

Father Rino Theriault was the new Rector at St. Andre. Although we had been classmates for eleven years at College St. Louis and at the University of Laval, he was not a relative but was a good friend. He allowed the use of the Chapel of St. Eloi, a mission of St. Andre parish, with a seating capacity of about 75 people. Rina and I were very pleased with the arrangement and the venue because the little chapel on top of the village of Comeau Ridge was charming.

The Vatican, of course, has many rules for priests who get married. As mentioned, one being the attendance; it must be very private consisting of the couple, two witnesses and the priest blessing their marriage. Rina and I had many friends and relatives who wanted to attend our marriage and word got around that we could not invite them, but we were getting married at Chapel St. Eloi on Saturday April 16th at 5:00 P.M. The day of our wedding a storm dropped five inches of snow on the community but nonetheless 125 packed into the little chapel with clearly a great deal of standing. After the marriage we went to the Recreation Centre and another 200 descended upon us.

This very same weekend the bishop was having his yearly visit to the Parish of St. Andre and celebrated mass Sunday morning at St. Eloi; 12 attended. The bishop, knowing about the events of the previous day wretchedly commented about the divisiveness of the two events.

I continued my professional life as Psychology Professor, and I had a private practice of Clinical Psychology. Since ordination all my earnings went to help the education of my brothers and sisters and for my group homes. This stipend was now unnecessary because, as previously mentioned; the province was now opening group homes through the Department of Social Services. I was gratified my private group home was the vanguard of this noble practice of aiding wayward children. My small contribution led the way to a humanely and Christian movement.

When we married Rina was fifty and I fifty-four. We stayed in the old farmhouse. Like couples in their twenties, we were starting our future together with almost zero assets. Unlike most newlyweds, however, I had a good paying job. Finances were not a worry. In 1991 I signed a contract as Clinical Psychologist for parolees of Correctional Services Canada. The majority of the parolees were sex offenders. I was getting deeper and deeper into the murky world of sex offenders and victims.

Not long after our marriage the Rector of Assumption parish sent a lady to ask why I was not attending church. It was generally known her school teaching husband was homosexual, or bisexual, and was caught by her in bed with his male friend. I was appalled by the rector and the pitiable lady thinking I could tolerate seeing her husband serving at the altar (but not celebrating), reading from the Bible and preaching from the altar when I was ostracized and vilified for getting married; getting married after thirty years of service to the very same diocese. The hypocrisy of it all!

Another disconcerting incident occurred when my niece asked if I could preach at her wedding. I told her the rector would never allow it. She confided she had a plan he wouldn't be able to refuse. She apparently first asked the rector if her fiancée's boss, an ex-priest, could say the English reading. The priest acquiesced. She then asked if another uncle, an ex-priest, could say the French reading. The priest assented. Her next request was to have a layman give the sermon. He answered to the affirmative as long as the non-cleric had learned the formation from attending religious teachings like *L'Ecole de la Foi*. My niece responded the layman had even taught at *L'Ecole de la Foi*. The rector was delighted with that answer but queried as to the layman's name.

"My Uncle Leo?"

"Oh no, I can't accept him, he's an ex-priest."

"You just accepted my intended's boss and my other uncle who are both ex-priests."

"Yes, but they left the diocese when they got married, Leo did not." Apparently, a priest who married not only deserved expulsion from the Church but also from the community as well. The hypocrisy of it all!

When my father died in 1995, I asked the rector if I could give the sermon at his funeral. Of course, it was refused. General Boucher could attend mass for his sister, in the same parish, when awaiting trial for child molestation, but not I. It would seem a priest getting married is worse than a priest sexually molesting altar boys and stealing the parish's money. The hypocrisy of it all!

After our marriage some fellow priests put me on their blacklist. General Boucher was one of them. Any time we met I would greet him cordially, but he was distant and obviously embarrassed. His body language was clear, but he never verbalized his emotions. He was judgmental regarding my marriage, but he never cleared his own back yard. When he was indicted for sexual assault in 1995, some of my friends who were altar boys in 1947 told me he was sexually molesting altar boys way back then. He had the audacity of being condescending to me for getting married while his own closet was dark as hades. The hypocrisy!

How many altar boys did he molest? We will never know. After 45 years of priesthood the number of victims would probably be shocking. He reminded me of Joe Paul Levesque who baptized me; very judgmental of others but unrepented of his own deception and fallaciousness. He managed to climb the social ladder to the rank of Brigadier General, head of the Catholic Canadian Army and Monsignor while being bad tempered and a pedophile.

At his funeral in 2010 in St. Michael's, Drummond, NB the following ministry was in attendance:

Bishop Claude Champagne officiated, assisted by Bishop Emeritus Gérard Dionne, Msgr. Urbain Lang, Msgr. Eymard Desjardins, Fathers Pierre Thibodeau, Frédéric Poitras, Roland Poitras, Ivan Thériault, Jean Bourgeois, W.L. Magdziak, Alfred Ouellet, Georges Fournier, Aurèle Godbout, Normand Godbout, Roger Dionne, Lucien Lévesque, Rino Thériault, Jean-Marie Martin, Gilbert Doddatto, Gaëtan Côté, Claude Côté, and Bertrand Ouellet.

The hypocrisy of it all!

Before our marriage I was in constant demand to preside over marriages and funerals. After my marriage I became persona non grata, not accepted in the church, so I was asked for eulogies at funeral parlors or for Christian messages at wedding receptions. I felt I was still doing ministry but outside traditional methods. This rang true when an anecdote was given after a eulogy. A member of the deceased family thanked me and said I had not lost my touch; my touch for the oratory and for the scripture. He continued that the Catholic Church reminded him of a farmer who has good modern machinery in the shed, but stubbornly uses his horse and plow. The Church hierarchy seems more interested in protecting its power than in the welfare of its people. It has forgotten Jesus' Parable of the Lost Sheep (Mathew 18:12-14 and Luke 15:3-7) whereby a shepherd leaves his flock of 99 in order to find one that is lost.

The hypocrisy of it all!

By getting married I knew I would be extricated from the ministry of the church but it didn't mean, however, I had to agree with either the policy or the execution. There is an old adage that states, "Priest one day, priest forever." Or put another way, you can kick a priest out of priesthood, but you cannot kick the priesthood out of the priest. The hypocrisy of it all!

It takes four years of university studies followed by another four years of Grand Seminary studies in Theology and Spirituality to become a priest. This is accompanied by very strict moral, spiritual and physical discipline that is often decried as brainwashing. Leaving the priesthood is like losing a life companion to divorce or death. It is not an easy decision. For many priests the decision is almost impossible. Often, due to their circumscribed education, they don't have another discipline to fall back on to earn a living. They are stuck in the priesthood and their maid becomes a life companion and the church looks the other way. The hypocrisy of it all!

Archbishop Robichaud pointed his finger in my face and said priests like me were destroying the church. My studies in psychology gave me a professional independence he could not accept, yet he would not protect the children of his diocese from pedophile priests. Priests who studied in fields other than theology appeared to be a threat to him, a threat to his authority. He was so different from Bishop Gagnon of Edmundston and one of my professors at Laval Grand Seminary who recommended we further our studies after ordination and better yet to have master's degrees in different fields rather than a Doctorate in one. He felt priests often got too close to the trees and lost sight of the forest; studying different disciplines should be enrichment not a liability. Similarly, marriage broadens one's horizon and is an asset and not a liability. After four years of study, a

REVELATIONS: THE TRUE STORY OF REV. DR. JOSEPH LEO THERIAULT

master's degree in Divinity and thirty years of pastoral work, I felt I was an asset not a liability to the church. Unfortunately, Archbishop Robichaud felt differently. The hypocrisy of it all!

"I have no choice, Leo, and I understand you are a superb preacher. I've heard many parents say they wake their kids for Mass and if you're giving the sermon they're up and anxious to attend. Now, that's a gift you have many would envy."

"The fact of the matter, your Excellency, if I sleep with my maid, I can continue my ministry. If I were in love with another man, I could keep my ministry. If I molested altar boys, I could continue as a priest. If I get married, I'm persona non grata in the church. Don't you think this is hypocrisy?"

Chapter XVI

CORRECTIONAL SERVICES
1991-1996

While I was Professor of Psychology at the University of Moncton, I was also a contract psychologist for prison parolees in the province. In sequence, after retiring from the University I was the French therapist for French sex offenders of North West New Brunswick. This was a federal-provincial group therapy program. I ran 14-week programs consisting of two half-day sessions a week mainly using the Relapse Prevention Model. Relapse Prevention is a cognitive-behavioral approach originally developed for the treatment of addictions. The Abstinence Violation Effect is a pivotal relapse prevention construct describing one's cognitive and affective response to re-engaging in a prohibited behavior.

Five years in these positions were an eye opener into the world of sex abuse. One can hardly believe the actuality of events whereby the victims have little possibility for a sanguine life.

Each victim has his or her individual dynamic reaction to their abuse.

CASE 1: PAM

Pam was previously mentioned in Chapter XI. She was raped by a priest when only twelve years old and when she told her mother she was slapped, called a liar and an evil girl. She turned to her mother for help and instead got a reprimand. She lived up to her mother's expectations by turning to alcohol, drugs and sexual promiscuity. She killed her baby girl believing she was protecting her from a similar hell. Seven years later she killed her husband wondering why she destroyed the ones she loved.

CASE 2: SYLVIE TURCOTTE

The National Film Board of Canada filmed *Le trou dans le mur* (The Hole in the Wall), a story about Sylvie Turcotte. Sylvie related being sexually abused by her father as far back as she could remember. When her father was molesting her she found mental refuge in a knot hole in the wall of her room. She later got married and had two boys. She didn't want boys because she feared they would become monsters like her father. For help she resorted to her sister who too had been abused by their father. Unlike Sylvie, she didn't want girls; she didn't want them to go through the same living hell as herself. Her first baby was a girl and she told the doctor to push it back in until it grew a penis. Two sisters who went through similar sexual abuse developed very dissimilar nightmares.

CASE 3: ANNIE

Five sisters in one family were sexually abused by their father. At age 19 one of the girls, let us say Annie, reported the abuse to her mother who called her a liar and a slut. Her sisters echoed their mother. Annie finally rebelled and reported him to Social Services. Hell broke loose and her whole family turned against her. Her sisters denied being molested by their father and called Annie a liar and a slattern. Her father denied his debauchery. The incident went to court, the father found guilty, served his time, put on parole, and referred to me for family counseling.

I met Annie in my office alone for about ten sessions before I allowed a group meeting. Annie was a mental catastrophe; insecure and scared to death to meet her parents. I had to strengthen her self-worth, self-confidence and resolve before meeting with her family for counseling.

I met her father and mother together after my second session with Annie and her mother asked when we would have a session with Annie. I told her Annie was not yet prepared for a group session and the mother furiously told me it was useless to meet without her. She screeched she wanted to confront her about her lies. I told her she could stay home if she wished but her husband was mandated to attend session. She did, nonetheless, continue attending meetings. She unrelentingly called Annie a slut but couldn't understand why her daughter was so sexually promiscuous?

Annie told me her father started fondling her when she was very young. He would take the girls to bed, kneel, say their prayers as one and then get into bed together. He would then put his hand under the blankets and fondle the girl on his side of the bed. She reported that none of the girls wanted to sleep on his side of the bed. He took advantage of his daughters whenever he could manipulate a rendezvous; behind the shed doing chores, fishing on the farm, when mother was shopping. It went on for years. When Annie became physically mature, she was very promiscuous and had sex at every opportunity; she felt if she became pregnant the odds would be against her having her father's baby.

I called a family session when Annie felt strong enough to meet her parents. Annie sat as close to me as was possible looking every bit a frightened five year old. Her mother was outwardly angry, staring at Annie and if eyes could kill Annie would be dead. Her father sat quietly with body language of an uneducated moron. I was prepared for a three-hour session because I was facing an angry mother, a scared daughter and a father in denial. I proffered different sexual incidents like night prayers and fishing rendezvous. Her father denied all feigning memory loss.

I then tabled an incident whereby the family apparently argued about Annie's sexual promiscuity. Her father curtailed the dispute by taking Annie to a friend's house. Regrettably he made a detour through the woods and had sex with her. I asked him if he remembered the event. He said he remembered the visit to their neighbors but not the detour through the bush. I suggested he must have been very drunk if he couldn't remember the detour and he immediately took this as an out and confessed he must have been because he didn't remember.

A light bulb must have gone on because Annie's mother now strangely accepted the truth as related by Annie. She told Annie she was a lucky girl. Annie questioned why she considered her lucky when she was raped by her father. Her mother replied she was lucky because she had Father Leo to help her when she herself never had anyone to help her. She then confided she was molested by her father, Annie's grandfather. They fell into each other's arms and cried. The mother then began blaming herself for leaving their home to work. I asked Annie if her father only took advantage of her when her mother was away, and she replied to the negative. Most of the molestation occurred when their mother was home.

When thus confronted the father admitted his offenses but added he had been forgiven by his parish priest. He blamed his heinous activity on his illiteracy and stupidity. I rejoined he had tremendous guile to sexually molest five daughters without each knowing the others were being molested, and under their mother's eyes. One had to be shrewd to have such cunning. Self-pity was not in the equation.

The pedophile is a predator and the victim doesn't have a chance.

The family was from General Boucher's parish of St. Quentin. After her husband was accused and found guilty of incest, the woman confided to me Father Boucher became very nasty towards the whole family, especially her. She even left the church choir to avoid his nasty encounters. The whole episode was very painful but doubly so when she needed the support of her parish priest and all she got was admonishment. Perhaps this incestuous family surfaced repressed memories from the past. Perhaps Boucher was seeing himself as this incestuous father. We will never know.

CASE 4: RACHEL

Rachel was another case whereby she and her four sisters were molested by their father and did not know about each other's misfortunes. Each girl may have thought they were "special" with their father thereby keeping their secret. Rachel left adolescence and got married and had three children. She watched her father like a hawk fearing he would molest her children, his grandchildren. One day she told her sister she felt her niece seemed to be having behavioral problems at school, acting as she had at age ten. She continued that she acted up in school because she was sexually molested by their father. Her sister was shocked and admitted she too had been sexually assaulted. They checked with the other three sisters and all admitted having sexual intercourse with their father. Regardless of their sentry, they discovered three of their father's granddaughters were being sexually molested by their father as well.

They reported their father's evil activities to Social Services of New Brunswick and, surprisingly, when he was arrested, he admitted his guilt and was sentenced to serve time in prison.

Pedophiles are expert predators. In this case it took the granddaughter's misbehavior at school to surface the abuse.

It is very unusual for sex offender to admit their crimes. My personal experience determined at least 85% of offenders deny and accuse.

Annie's entire family turned against her due to denial, humiliation and shame. Rachel's case was the antithesis; all pulled together, admitted the fact and placed the blame where it belonged, on their father.

Pedophiles are predators, victims powerless but truth will set them free.

CASE 5: JANE.

Jane was ten years old living with her mother who had many male friends. One evening while her mother was in the bedroom with such a friend, Jane was alone with another "waiting in line." Jane felt comfortable and secure with him because he seemed very nice and her mother liked him. Jane felt her mother preferred and liked her boyfriend's better than she.

The "nice man" asked Jane if she would like to play an adult game. She accepted. He fondled her. She bled but it did not scare her as she felt close to him. It was a warming sensation, a feeling of acceptance. The adult game made her feel mature. It was a onetime incident, however, because he refused to repeat this so-called adult game and Jane felt rejected.

I counseled her when she was sixteen and on probation for using drugs. Her addiction seemed to have been caused by her family environment more than by her one sexual experience at the age of ten. The root cause of her turbulent life was nonetheless sexually related.

It is clinically believed about fifty percent of child victims of sexual abuse manage to overcome their oppression without long term trauma. The fifty percent that do suffer, however, suffer badly and are far too many.

CASE 6: JOE.

In 1995 Joe was found guilty of incest with his daughter and was sentenced to prison for nine months. When on parole he was referred to me for counseling. He told me his wife cheated on him while he was in prison; she continued denying it even though he maintained he had proof. After he repeatedly told me this accusation, I asked him for his proof. He held his ground but wouldn't reveal his source of information. Someone must have told him the tale because, after all, he was behind bars.

I then remembered another local was in prison at the same time as Joe. He was alleged to have told fellow inmates a woman's vagina had to be penetrated at least once a month otherwise it would seal up. Many inmates believed this stupid know-it-all who talked with such authority, and Joe was one. Joe had heard the story before he went to prison from the same imbecile.

I asked Joe if his proof was due to his wife's vagina not being sealed. He ashamedly admitted he heard the blowhard's bombast on sex.

The crux of the matter was these absurd dissertations by a lunatic were an excuse for Joe to sexually molest his daughter, believing he was rendering her a great service by preventing the sealing of her vagina.

The rationalization of offenders is simply amazing.

CASE 7: BOB.

Bob admitted having sexually abused five adolescent girls before being reported. During the Relapse Prevention Program, he queried why he only molested girls and not boys; he had been molested by his uncle.

"How old were you when your uncle abused you?"

"Ten years old."

"How old was victim number one?"

"Nine years old."

"How old was victim number two?"

"Ten years old."

"How old was victim number three?"

"Ten."

"How old was victim number four?"

"Nine."

"How old was victim number five?"

"Nine."

For a moment Bob was speechless. He was sexually attracted to nine and ten-year-old girls; girls that happened to be the same age as he when victimized. It was as if a part of his sexual maturation froze at age ten. This is called a developmental freeze and is like fetishism. Fetishism is a psychosexual abnormality in which an individual's sexual impulse becomes fixated on a sexual symbol rather than the basic love object. The fixation can be articles of underclothing, hats, shoes, gloves or the object may be a bodily part such as hair, hair color, hands, thighs, feet, legs, ears, eyes or size of breasts. Others still may be fixated on the age of the victim.

One middle-aged offender who was fixated on adolescent girls was asked why he preferred adolescents to adults. Almost in ecstasy, he answered it was like comparing fresh vegetables from the garden to old vegetables sitting on the shelf for a week.

CASE 9: SHARON.

Sharon came to me for counseling because she was sexually confused. Her inner self felt like a ten-year-old. This inner child was naked, cold and crying. Sharon wanted to know who the girl was. During a counseling session she realized she was the inner girl, and she then curled into the fetal position and screamed in pain. The pain was as if giving birth.

At ten, Sharon's father had her undress and started fondling her. She resisted and refused to obey him. He then put her in the dark and cold vegetable cellar under the house. All these years she repressed the incident into her subconscious, but the little girl kept returning to haunt her. Once consciously understanding the realism of the event she underwent tremendous physical and psychosomatic pain as if in childbirth, freeing her body from the inner child.

Once realized and relieved, Sharon was able to go about her life as a normal adult.

CASE 10: SUE.

In later years I was a consultant to the Arizona, USA Child Protective Services (CPS).

Sue's father had been found guilty of sexually molesting her when she was just fourteen. His inadequate sentence was one-year probation and a no communication restraining order until she was legally an adult. Sue was put under the care of the CPS and only one year on her father brought CPS to court to cancel the restraining order and permission to contact his daughter. I was called to testify as an expert in the field.

The night before court, her father threw a newspaper clipping onto my front yard; an article about a victim lying in court about her persecution. As he drove away, he yelled, "She will lie tomorrow."

The following day at court his attorney presented the statement that Sue had denied she smoked when in fact she did. He opined she lied then therefore she is lying now. He continued, without statistics, that many victims do lie about their molestation. When during cross-examination he asked if I knew if some victims lied. I replied that statistics prove no more than five to ten percent of victims lie but 80 to 85% of sex offenders lie about their molestation. Using these statistics, offenders lie about 12 times more than do victims.

Unfortunately, the "lie defense" is very effective. It is used extensively by offenders and lawyers alike in court knowing full well the best defense is an offense. Victims, often juveniles, are at a disadvantage. Almost to a man, predators put blame and guilt on their prey; be they priests, coaches, teachers, parents, or scout leaders. The transgressors are experts at the game of deception.

This time, however, deception didn't work, and the plaintiff was refused contact.

The same attorney had two similar cases pending but when he heard I was to be a character witness for the plaintiffs he had his clients plead guilty.

These cases are not comprehensive but illustrate nonetheless how each victim has their own way of dealing with sexual molestation. Each is unique. Some victims will not be overly traumatized while others will murder or consider suicide. Children should not have to experience and live through such consequences for the rest of their lives.

The Church has not always been the Good Shepherd as it should be; often the antithesis. Some popes have likewise not been above the evil fray. Pope Julius III who presided over the second session of the Counsel of Trent (1545-1563) had a sexual liaison with a 15-year-old boy he made cardinal. Julius III was promoting priest celibacy while practicing ephebophilia (an extension of pedophilia to puberty or adolescence).

Chapter XVII

TRUTH AND CONSEQUENCES

I n 1997 I made a thesis presentation at the University of Ottawa titled *Issues in Treating Sexual Offender Clergymen*.

I: SCOPE OF THE CURRENT CRISIS

The media headlines are clear: "TWELVE PRIESTS ABUSE STUDENTS"; "PRIEST ABUSE ONE HUNDRED STUDENTS"; "PRIEST HEADS SEX CLUB FOR ADOLESCENTS"; "ARCHDIOCESE OF TEXAS COURT-ORDERED TO PAY $119 MILLION IN FINE AND DAMAGE"; "DIOCESE OF NEW MEXICO NEAR BANKRUPTCY HAVING TO PAY $51 MILLION FOR PRIESTS' SEXUAL OFFENDERS." In Arizona a priest had a list of over 400 names of boys he had sexually abused over a period of 25 years and they were all rated on their sexual efficiency on a scale of 1 to 10.

And the list goes on.

Pedophilia according to DSM-IV (Data and Statistical Manual of Mental Disorder) is "…recurrent, intense, sexual urges and sexually arousing fantasies, of at least six months duration, involving sexual activity with a prepubescent child. The person has acted on these urges, or is markedly distressed by them. The age of the child is generally 13 or younger. The age of the person is arbitrarily set at 16 or older and at least 5 years older than the child."

A. Nicholas Groth, PhD in *The Child Molester* added a new dimension in classifying pedophiles as:

Regressed: erotically attracted to both adults and children, stressful situations with an age-peer will trigger pedophile tendencies.

Fixated: experience no sexual attraction toward adults. Manifest an arrest in their psychosexual development.

Ephebophilia being the primary sexual interest in mid to late adolescents, generally ages 15 to 19. It is not mentioned as such in the DSM-IV. Many sexual offender clergymen, however, do fall in this group according to Aquinas Walter Richard Sipe, author, and erstwhile American Benedictine monk-priest.

Studies indicate child molesters commit an average of 60 offenses for every incident that comes to public attention; 20 to 25% of women and 10% of men experienced sexual abuse during childhood or adolescence. A research in 1989 revealed that 5.5% of male psychologists, 0.6% of female psychologists and 6.4% of psychiatrists admitted having sex with clients. 1.6% of clients revealed having sexual involvement with therapist or analyst (Sipe 1995).

Sexual involvement is therefore a reality in the counseling profession and is not exclusivity to one profession or another.

II: CODE OF SEXUAL ETHICS FOR PRIESTS (SIPE 1995)

Until recently clergymen were the teachers of right and wrong. What else was needed? Do what you preach, but the past 50 years are proving that such is not the case. Clergymen are not any different than professionals in other helping and healing professions. The Hippocratic Oath contains an explicit prohibition against sexual relations with patients but some physicians still break the rule.

> Whoever welcomes a child such as this for my sake welcomes me, and whoever welcomes me welcomes, not me but him who sent me. – Mark 9, 36-37

> Anyone who is an obstacle to bring down one of these little ones who have faith in me would be better drowned in the depths of the sea with a great millstone around his neck. – Matt 18, 5-7

There is no equivocation about the inappropriateness of an adult's sexual activity with a child. Yet, religiosity is very common among pedophiles of all faiths. These clergymen use their position of trust and presumption of moral integrity as a cover for their sexual activity with children and adolescents.

CHURCH'S TEACHING ON SEXUALITY

When asked why the American bishops were having such a difficult time dealing with priest sexual abusers, one bishop responded, "Undoubtedly part of the problem is that some of the bishops themselves are abusers." (Sipe 1995).

In 2000 years no Christian church has developed an adequate theology of sexuality specifying the nature and place of sexuality within the scheme of salvation and theological system. The Roman Catholic's official teaching on sex is that all directly sought or welcomed sexual pleasure outside marriage is gravely sinful and that every act of sexual intercourse within marriage must remain open to the transmission of life.

SEXUAL BEHAVIOR OF PRIESTS DURING CONFESSION (SIPE 1990).

A number of priests reported having a spontaneous ejaculation and others reported masturbating. This behavior is clearly part of a pathological process.

ETHICS FOR CLERGYMEN

Professionally, it should be clear that sexual contact is never appropriate as part of any pastoral care or ministry. Sexual contact is not only sexual intercourse but includes fondling or any sexual touching, sexual innuendo, kissing and nudity.

All clergy can aspire to no less a professional standard than physicians. They require a level of maturity that can sustain a professional stance in all ministries and a degree of spirituality that can ensure sexually appropriate, responsible, and honest relationships with all women, men and children.

CONFUSION BETWEEN CONFIDENTIALITY AND SECRECY

Confidentiality is a private, personal, and privileged communication that must be protected at great sacrifice because it is in the service of personal transformation and growth. It may be necessary to protect due process.

Secrecy is a stance that reserves access to knowledge in the service of power, control or manipulation. Secrecy is often rationalized as the only way to avoid scandal.

III – WHICH PRIESTS ABUSE MINORS? (SIPE 1995)

Seventy to eighty percent of priests who sexually abuse have themselves been abused as children, some by priests. Furthermore, a high percentage of those who later abused youngsters – whether or not they themselves were abused as children – were in effect given permission for such activity by a priest or religious superior who himself crossed the sexual boundary with the priest abuser during the time he was studying for ordination. Ten percent of priests report that they were approached sexually by a priest during the time of their theological studies.

For a shy, sexually inhibited man such silent and secret gratification from a superior offers bonding, release and acceptance of rationalization all at the same time. He finds himself in a balancing act inconsistent with religious integrity and sexual responsibility.

Four categories of factors seem to explain the pedophile behavior:

1. Genetic factors seem to predispose the individual. Some pedophiles seem to be genetically limited in their psychosexual devel-

opment as some individuals do not develop intellectually beyond the level of a child or adolescent.

2. Psychodynamic factors. They seem normal genetically but psychic factors can arrest someone at one stage of development.

3. Social/Situational factors. These priests have a problem with celibacy but love their Church and priesthood, they are devoted. They play by the Church's rules. Their behavior is not compulsively driven. They are like the product of the system.

4. Moral factors. One should rather say a moral or absence of morality. They coldly, calculatingly, by design involve themselves sexually with minors because they want to. They choose it, not compulsively, indiscriminately, or impulsively. They are very seldom caught, they are too calculating, they pick their partners carefully, as a person cheating on his/her spouse. They will stop at nothing to protect themselves. When caught they have a great propensity to suicide.

The problem of sexual abuse by clergymen is neither new nor limited to Roman Catholic priests.

IV – CHURCH'S AWARENESS

Jean-Jacques Rousseau writes about an experience he endured at a retreat center in 1725.

The Marquis Donatien de Sade was introduced to sex by his priest uncle in 1762.

Mount Cashell Orphanage, run by the Congregation of Christ in St. John's, Newfoundland and Labrador, response to sexual abuse in the in the 1980s. "Father is only human. He is a sick man. He is a poor 74 year old priest."

In America the problem of priest sexual abuse was addressed publicly for the first time at a meeting held on the campus of Notre-Dame University in 1967. All American bishops were invited to that meeting. (Sipe 1995).

In 1983 Father Thomas Doyle was sent to investigate the diocese of Lafayette. Its bishop had known as early as 1974 that one of his priests was abusing children. In 1985 Father Doyle along with a priest psychiatrist and a lawyer produced a report on the problem of child sexual abuse by priests and made it available to the bishops. This report, which accurately predicted the events of the next ten years, was largely ignored or rejected by the majority of the bishops at the time of its release.

The church's traditional preference for secrecy has been assaulted irrevocably by the facts revealed in press and courtrooms. Prior to 1988, church authorities handled problems of child abuse in secrecy. Since 1988, under the pressure of lawsuits, the picture changed, but still one bishop to a priest, there is no real problem. The devil is just persecuting the church in this way. The church's response has been denial, secrecy and reluctance to discuss.

V – CHILD SEXUAL ABUSE INTERVENTION AND TREATMENT ISSUES (SIPE 1995)

Some pedophiles will recognize their urge as inappropriate, become fearful of the behavior it demands, and avoid compromising situations for years. They may ask for treatment, but most active child molesters do not turn themselves in for therapy because they do not experience any guilt in connection with it. Some confide their sins in confession, which perpetuates a cycle of guilt and relief and seals their behavior behind the sacred wall of secrecy. They believe they have sinned but the confessional expunges their evil deeds. Others are amoral, anti-social psychopaths that fear no guilt.

Some church authorities do not like the intervention of counselors with their pedophile clergy which can be a very difficult issue for the counselor.

VI – TREATMENT MODALITIES

The Twelve Step Model
Dr. Patrick Carnes, author of *Out of the Shadows* (1983) and *Don't Call it Love* (1991) uses a model for addiction similar to that developed by Alcoholic Anonymous.

STEP I: *We admitted we are powerless over sex and that our lives have become unmanageable.*

Step One confronts the paradox of our addictive and coaddictive processes. We feel powerful when, in fact, we are powerless and need help.

STEP II: *Came to believe that a Power greater than ourselves could restore us to sanity.*

Step Two challenges our grandiosity and reminds us that we are limited human beings.

STEP III: *Made a decision to turn our will and our lives over to the care of God as we understand Him.*

Step Three underlines our efforts to control when we need to take responsibility only for ourselves and leave the rest to our Higher Power.

STEP IV: *Made a searching and fearless moral inventory of ourselves.*

Step Four takes the energy out of the shame that separates us from ourselves, others, and our Higher Power. It brings acceptance.

STEP V: *Admitted to God, to ourselves, and to another human being the exact nature of our wrongs.*

Step Five asks us to break through the paralyzing fear that prevents us from receiving forgiveness and faith.

STEP VI: *Were entirely ready to have God remove all these defects of character.*

Step Six attacks our perfectionism, allowing us to experience our wounds so that we might heal.

STEP VII: *Humbly asked Him to remove our shortcomings.*

Step Seven asks us to give up our willingness so that we might allow change to work in our lives and to begin grieving.

STEP VIII: *Made a list of all persons we had harmed, and became willing to make amends to them all.*

Step Eight asks to exchange our pride for honesty.

STEP IX: *Made direct amends to such people wherever possible, except when to do so would injure them or others.*

Step Nine challenges us to stop seeking approval and to pursue integrity by making amends for harm we have caused.

STEP X: *Continued to take personal inventory and when we were wrong promptly admitted it.*

Step Ten makes a daily prescription to set aside our defenses and admit our errors.

STEP XI: *Sought through prayer and meditation to improve our conscious contact with God as we understand Him, praying only for knowledge of His will for us and the power to carry that out.*

Step Eleven asks us to trade the magical thinking of escapism for the realities of spiritual life even though they are difficult.

STEP XII: *Having had a spiritual awakening as a result of these steps, we tried to carry this message to sex offenders, and to practice these principles in all our affairs.*

Step Twelve tells us to trade in our martyr-like victim roles and share the changes in our lives with others with similar problems.

VII – SYMPTOMS AND BEHAVIORS

Additionally, based on his research, Carnes (1992) has identified ten symptoms and behaviors that he believes indicate the presence of sexual addiction:

1. A pattern of out of control behavior

2. Severe consequences due to sexual behavior

3. Inability to stop despite adverse consequences

4. Persistent pursuit of self-destructive or high-risk behavior

5. Ongoing desire to or effort to limit sexual behavior

6. Sexual obsession and fantasy as a primary coping strategy

7. Increasing amounts of sexual experience (because the current level of activity is no longer sufficient)

8. Severe mood changes around sexual activity

9. Inordinate amounts of time spent in obtaining sex, being sexual, or recovering from sexual experience

10. Neglect of important social, occupational, or recreational activities due to sexual behavior

To find balance in our lives, Dr. Carnes also recommends AA's Serenity Prayer, "God, grant me the serenity to accept the things I cannot change, courage to change the things I can, and wisdom to know the difference."

Relapse Prevention Model is cognitive behavioral model used extensively throughout North America. The utilization of relapse prevention strategies has become a crucial component of theory for recurring and somewhat intractable disorders. In recent years a number of clinicians and researchers have argued the treatment of sexual offenders ought to be based on an understanding of the process of relapse. The high recidivism rates of sexual offenders have led many theorists and researchers to view sexual deviance as analogous to addiction.

Doctors have the Hippocratic Oath but counselors, psychologists, politicians, lawyers and clergy have none.

Chapter XVIII

CHAIN OF EVENTS

In 1995 I assumed the position as director of a pilot project at the Madawaska Regional Correctional Centre; a federal-provincial group therapy program for French speaking sexual offenders. The project laid-out a 14-week program consisting of two half-day sessions a week mainly using the Relapse Prevention Model.

Relapse Prevention is a cognitive-behavioral approach to relapse with the goal of identifying and preventing high-risk situations such as substance abuse, obsessive-compulsive behavior, sexual offending, obesity, and depression. The Relapse Prevention Model defines a set of cognitive and behavioral strategies that can prevent or limit relapse episodes. These interventions are both immediate determinants and covert antecedents of relapse and include approaches such as skill training, cognitive restructuring and lifestyle changes.

We had three groups with a total of 31 offenders at the Centre. The offenders who disclosed first also seemed to come up with excellent relapse-prevention plans; their prognosis was very good.

An incident very similar to Sue's case in chapter XVI, Correctional Services, involved a wrongdoer who had been found guilty of sexually molesting his ten-year-old daughter. He subsequently could only see his daughter in the presence of an adult. Two years later I received a call from Social Services asking me if I could go to court in Edmundston to testify as an expert in the field of sexual abuse. This incestuous father was asking permission to see his daughter without the presence of an adult. I attended court once again.

The perpetrator's lawyer began by questioning my credentials. The court declared me an expert in the field of child abuse, but the plaintiff's lawyer kept attacking my expertise. Finally, the judge told him the court had declared me an expert in the field and he had to accept my expertise or be guilty of contempt of court. The lawyer then read my report whereby I mentioned his client was the first to disclose, had the best treatment plan and was one of the best participants in the Pathways program; ergo, with this prognosis his client should be allowed to privately see his daughter. I then asked my erstwhile client to read the first item of his relapse prevention plan. He read, "never to be alone with a minor."

I told the court a good relapse prevention plan had to be followed to its nth degree. I openly queried as to why a convicted pedophile would wish to be relieved from his relapse prevention plan unless he had ulterior motives. I went further and said if he is ever accused of pedophilia and if it is proven he was at any time alone with the victim, he should be declared guilty and sentenced accordingly. I continued children should never be alone with him without adult supervision and this goes for any pedophile.

One cannot judge a book by its cover. He had disclosed, participated very well and came up with an excellent relapse prevention plan. A nice cover, but the content did not match the jacket as we saw two years later. He played the game very well. He told us what we wanted to hear, but never internalized any values. He didn't have any remorse. We had seen the trauma of victims of pedophilia. We had seen the need of self-control. He didn't.

Self-control is paramount as it is in any addiction. If this father really loved his daughter, he would respect her and protect her from any danger, including himself. Sexual molestations don't just happen; they're proceeded by a chain of events that will lead to the assault. The perpetrator starts by grooming his or her victim or takes control by threatening bodily harm, even murder, or threatening family members. One must remember the pedophile is a predator and the victim usually a child. The victim is often powerless. The perpetrator usually proceeds by isolating the victim.

The offender in this instance was asking to be alone with his daughter thereby starting the chain of events that would again lead to an assault on his daughter. The book cover was the nice loving shepherd, but the content was the wolf who loved lamp chops. The father didn't have any repentance. He said he was sorry for what he had done but in reality he was sorry he had been caught or sorry for having lost his lamb chop.

Dissimilar to this case are participants who resist the therapy, reject disclosure but develop an acceptable relapse prevention plan and will not reoffend. They become conscious of the damage committed and get angry with themselves. They will then use the tools offered by the program and never victimize another quarry. The book cover may not be very good, but the book content is excellent. While some are working on the book jacket, others work on the content. They are not using the program as a game, a new tool to better hide his pedophilia, but an actual rehabilitation process.

Chapter XIX

FROM ROME TO LONDON

After my marriage in 1988 I was refused any activity in the Church. I could attend but not be active in any ceremony. The Anglican Church of Canada and the Roman Catholic Conference of Bishops of Canada had an agreement for the passage of priests from one denomination to the other. I decided in 1995 to take advantage of that agreement. It was two years prior to my retirement from the University and Rina and I were planning on retiring to Arizona to aid Rina's arthritic condition. I knew I could never fully retire so I figured I could assist in ministry in the US. In the meanwhile, I was accepted as an Anglican priest in the diocese of Fredericton. The bishop asked me to open a French service at the Anglican Church in Grand Falls. When I asked my father's opinion, he recommended I reconsider because I had lost too many friends when I ran for politics. I had earlier run for provincial legislative assembly as a conservative. At the time, conservatives were predominately anglophiles and my riding was French and Liberal. He was right, of course, but I felt if my friends could not accept my freedom of religion, they were not true friends.

Regardless, I ignored my father's warnings and went ahead with the bishop's request. I often pondered as to why I asked my father in the first place knowing full well his response and knowing full well I would go ahead anyway. I started using the French Episcopal Book of Common Prayer used in Quebec. It did not work. Although I was amicably accepted by priests from both churches, some influential members of the Anglican Church were not interested in having French services in their church, and most of the French who attended were pressured not to by their family or their priest and consequently ceased to further attend. We abandoned the idea of an Anglican French service and I then only served as fill-in for some Anglican priests until I moved to Arizona.

Since then, only over a span of 25 years or so, the Anglican church of Grand Falls has closed and four Roman Catholic churches have amalgamated into one with very low attendance, but the churches refuse to change. Tradition can be the flywheel of society, but it can also be a cog in the wheel of society.

In 1997 we retired to Arizona where I was licensed in the Episcopal Church and I did juvenile delinquent counseling. Besides celibacy, I found very little difference between the Roman Catholic Church, the Anglican Church and the Episcopal Church. I personally love the sacraments in all three.

In June of 2003 I was appointed in charge of the mission church in Kingman Arizona. It did not last long. Even at my extended age, I was still naïve. We had just gone to war in Iraq and either due to naïvetés or principle I polarized the small congregation by saying it was an immoral war because the terrorists of 9/11 were from Saudi Arabia and not Iraq. After only three months I had to resign and I returned to juvenile counseling; my true love where I felt I was of greater use. I was helping the victims of society. I felt I was living Luke 15:7 whereby Jesus said, "I tell you that in the same way there will be more rejoicing in heaven over one sinner who repents than over ninety-nine righteous persons who do not need to repent."

In 1997 I wrote and passed the state exam for Professional Counselors License and got down to seriously pursue a position. After an extensive search, many refusals and promises I finally found an opening in New Arizona Family. It was, and is, a long-term residential treatment center for alcoholics and drug addicts. Since all my working experience and studies to date were in French, I had trepidation as to my ability to work in English. I consequently accepted the job with a very low salary – mostly to test my efficiency in English. I was surprised and gratified with my ability and success in both group and individual counseling.

After about six months working at New Arizona Family, I received a call from the Director of Child Protective Services in Kingman. She had been court ordered to provide individual and family counseling to a ten-year old boy and his adoptive parents. The judge specified the counselor should be licensed by the Arizona State Counseling Examination Board and could not be a counselor from the local Mental Health Clinic. She had apparently searched for a counselor in the contiguous towns to no avail. She then contacted the State Licensing Board and was told I was qualified and possibly available. I told her I was interested but would not accept the position for only one client a week and she accepted my request. The salary was seven times more than I could get from a private counseling corporation and added to my qualifications.

While counseling the family as indicated, I checked with the Department of Correctional Services, and the Director of Juvenile Corrective Services told me he was looking for a new counselor. He hired me on a trial basis and in no time I was counseling four days a week. My clients had a hard time with my French name so at Child Protective Services (CPS) they called me "Dr. T" and at Juvenile Corrections I was called "Dr. Leo."

At CPS I ended up counseling the same boy that brought me to Kingman in the first place. He had been adopted at ten, but his new parents were not told of the severity of abuse he had previously encountered. For a few months his new environment and parents kept him under control, but past misbehavior resurfaced, and his mother could not handle his disruptive conduct – breaking objects, beating their dog, striking his adoptive mother, ad infinitum. He was uncontrollable. The adoptive parents asked for professional help but felt the assistance they were given was far from professional. In Arizona in 1997 anyone could write counselor on a shingle, hang it on their door and accept patients; consequently, too often clients were treated by unprofessional quacks.

This seemed to be the situation with this unfortunate family. One day the adoptive mother succumbed into a diabetic coma and was ambulated to hospital, and while there the father brought the boy to CPS and left him there. The parents were brought to court by the CPS and charged for support. The mother explained their predicament, was understood and the court ordered CPS to have a licensed professional to help; the help was me. I counseled the family for a year and it seemed to have been a success because for the most part his disruptive behavior ceased and he got along well with his parents.

The Department of Correctional Services kept me busy for three to four days a week and I worked for them for 12 years. These years were most gratifying and I felt more like a priest counseling delinquent children and teenagers than I did doing parish work. Getting a lost sheep back on the straight and narrow is most rewarding. I used Client-Centered Therapy, Cognitive Therapy and Reality Therapy according to the case.

As previously mentioned, client-centered therapy, which is also known as person-centered, non-directive, or Rogerian therapy, is a counseling approach that requires the client to take an active role in his or her treatment with the therapist being nondirective but supportive. Cognitive therapy is a type of psychotherapy in which negative patterns of thought about the self and the world are challenged in order to alter unwanted behavior patterns or treat mood disorders such as depression. Reality therapy is a therapeutic approach that focuses on problem-solving and making better choices in order to achieve specific goals. Reality therapy is focused on the here and now rather than the past.

On my first session with a delinquent I always asked, "Do you know who Ronald Regan is? Do you know who Bill Clinton is? What do you think they have in common? Other than being presidents of the United States of course." Upon negative responses to their commonality, I'd tell them both had abusive fathers. My discourse continued that at their age they had life choices; they could sit on the pity pot for the rest of their lives complaining how abusive their father was, they could transfer their anger onto others, or they could decide not to allow the past ruin their future. One may not have liked their presidency, but one must admire their achievements. I attempted to teach they were responsible for their own actions and should not blame others. I listened to their past but didn't dwell on it by having them spend more time looking where they are going, or could go, rather than looking where they had been. I really enjoyed working with those teenagers as they were a real challenge. Success with them was very rewarding.

In early days a 14-year-old boy who was on probation for fighting, destruction of property and stealing was referred to me. He was considered mentally retarded. During the second session of counseling his demeanor and conversation made me feel only an above average intelligence. I therefore suspected a learned mentally retarded behavior. I checked with his probation officer to determine when and where he learned this behavior. Was it at home, in a boarding school or in an integrated classroom? I discovered he had been adopted along with a half-sister who was mentally retarded. For the third session I asked the mother to attend.

My first question was, "How old was Jim when you adopted him"?

She blushed and Jim said, "I have been adopted?"

"Yes, I also adopted your half-sister. You have the same mother."

She continued that she adopted Jim when he was 16 months old and had been in five foster homes. I knew a child being shunted from home to home during early developing stages is most harmful and a child develops distrust. I continued individual therapy with Jim until the end of his probation a year later. I felt he improved his self-image and self-dependency. His school grades improved and his misbehavior became negligible. He had been exposed to mental retardation in an integrated classroom as well as from his sister. Instead of being a role model for the handicapped, he took the handicapped as a role model for himself. He fooled all in authority. During counseling he tested me with negative transfers of his traumatic experiences, but I was onto his game. I let him express his feelings for three sessions without being judgmental and he finally realized I was not rejecting him but accepting him as he was. He was okay. My approach was transactional analysis in practice; a method of therapy wherein social transactions are analyzed to determine the self-esteem of the patient to enable the resolution of emotional problems. He finished his probation and five years hence he did not have a relapse.

A young girl was referred to me for having violent temper tantrums. Her father had committed suicide, but she wouldn't believe it. She fanaticized, she believed, her father was murdered by a drug cartel and the police flubbed the investigation. I met with her well dressed and well coiffured middle-class mother who admitted her husband had been involved in drug trafficking. She continued that her husband had exceedingly loved their only daughter and she couldn't understand why he took his own life knowing full-well it would hurt and perhaps damage her.

I had seen enough of the seedy side of life to know it was not uncommon for criminals in the drug business to settle arguments by threatening loved ones. I asked the widow if she felt her husband might have committed suicide to protect his daughter. She had never thought of this angle but gladly accepted the possibility.

Shortly thereafter I was in the probation office when our subject's probation officer received a call from her school director. She had thrown a horrific tantrum and the director threatened to call the police. I was on my way but when I arrived she had calmed down. I asked her if the director could stay as he might be able to help. She surprisingly agreed. I asked her what brought on her outburst just a short time ago. She said she didn't know. She just felt angry with the world. I talked about her father's suicide and she got very emotional, again blaming the justice system for not doing its job

I then explained the discussion I had with her mother, blaming the drug world for her father's death. I explained how deeply he had loved her, loved her so much that he took his own life to protect her. This explanation seemed to work. She was a bright girl and after our discussion her grades went up and there were no more behavior problems at school. She seemed to have mentally resolved her problems and gone forward with life.

The anger of this young girl is not unique among juvenile delinquents. Most have anger problems that must be addressed. Anger is a normal emotion, a survival reaction that was spawned by our caveman ancestors. It is generated by pain or fear. It is triggered by an attack or a threat to one's well-being. The response is fight or flight. Fight if you feel you can

105

destroy or eliminate the cause of suffering or fear. Flight if you feel you cannot overcome the cause of anxiety; flight into depression, denial, drug abuse, alcoholism, overachievement (workaholic), or any countless other escape routes. If you do not know or deny the cause of your anger, you will relocate it to someone or something else.

In this topic case, our young girl interpreted her father's suicide as a rejection and replaced this pain with anger. After realizing her father had not let her down but had given his life for her, there was no further need for displacement and she could go on with the normal grief of her father's death without attachment.

Another interesting case of anger was displayed by the younger of two brothers who were in and out of detention. They were well known to Juvenile Probation staff and city police. He was referred to me for counseling while in detention. He had an anger problem and was claustrophobic. At our first session he gave me a poem about his sister who had been killed by a hit and run drunk driver. It triggered an outburst of anger well described in this first poem

HE KILLED MY SISTER

Kill, maime, dismember, destroy
I'll play with your life like a childs toy.
A burning hatred down deep inside,
That only your blood could ever satisfy.
The torture of your death I soon begin
Not knowing remorse not feeling for sin
I will bite and tear into the flesh of your neck.
Start to giggle as I witness your body a wreck

After seven hours of counseling he wrote the following where he asks for strength to deal with his anger and forgiveness for the drunk driver.

THE POWER OF THE SWORD

Heavenly father please hear me tonight,
I need so much guidance to live my life right,
The pain that I hold is so hard to bare,
It often makes me not want to care,
At night time I pray, I pray to you lord,
I ask oh please Jesus, bless me with a sword,
A sword of such power to set anything free,
So I can free the Anger that has belt inside of me,

I do not know how to do this for my mind is not clear,
Or do I wish not to for I think it will bring only fear,
Because I think I am scared to free this painfull anger,
The anger that has been made by the one who put my sister in danger,
He should not of been drinking,
He left the scene speeding,
For that is what caused my sister to die from eternal bleeding,
I wonder if he knows how many people he has hurt,
I hope this has made him feel more lower than dirt,
Against him I want to commit the greatest of sins,
But if I did I know I wood not be the one to win,
I wish he wood have said sorry for what he has done,
I wood have meant a lot to more than just one,
But I know I now must forgive him for taking the one I now miss,
For forgiveness is the sword to free my anger and deal with the
death of my sis.
Forever may she
Rest in Peace

After twenty-five days and eleven hours of counseling, his newly acquired insight elicited his third poem.

THOUGHT OF A PRAYER

When I get angry it makes me upset,
I then do something to later regret,
But this time I'm gonna write a poem to help me,
It's gonna be my prayer to ask Jesus to sit me free,
I have never been able to manage my anger in the right way,
My anger don't allow me to think about what I do or say,
My anger has caused me to teach only negative to my brother,
Which will only lead to him later hurting my caring mother,
Because that is all I have done to her over the past couple years,
I have always been in jail never at home to share her cheers,
I have respected my friends more than my dad,
Been told this by him and only feld mad,
I have hurt my little sister, so many time made her sad,
Because I wood do crimes with my friends to feel Big and bad,
I have led my family through all this pain,
Because of the drug I wood put into my vein,
In the past I have thought of what I have done,
It made me come to the conclusion to pick up a gun,
I placed the cold steal into my mouth,

Then thought do I want to go North or South,
As I thought in my head is this for real,
I decided their's other ways for this wound to heel,
That's when I realized I have thought while I was mad,
But with this thought came happiness that made me sad,
Because I finally realized I'm making my life a crime,
And considering the people in it not worth as much as a dime,
Writing this poem has made me decide,
To get on that bus that gives god's ride,
Because I don't want to hurt my family again,
And I don't want to live my life in prison,
So I ask you dear Jesus please help my out,
And forgive me of my sins and send me about.

These poems fully illustrate the pain he felt over his sister's death – anger and destruction. He realized his anger was out of control and he needed help.

Counseling these teenagers was most rewarding. During my twelve years of counseling juvenile delinquents in Arizona I had many such rewarding experiences. I felt my work was as pastoral or as priestly as working in a parish. I have heard many times if a delinquent was incarcerated and was not a criminal when he went in, he would be one when he came out. There is some truth to this axiom but it doesn't tell the whole story. Juvenile delinquents tend to brag about their misbehavior and stretch the truth to the point of disbelief. When they are released they often try to emulate the toughness, bravado and recklessness of their detention idols. They also often want to make a "reputation" for themselves.

Chapter XX

WHAT DREAMS ARE MADE OF

When we first moved to Arizona, I contacted The Meadows in Wickenburg, Arizona, a private treatment center for men and women struggling with emotional trauma, addiction, and complex mental health issues. It has an excellent reputation throughout America and Europe and many celebrities use this facility. I was hoping for a part-time position.

One Sunday afternoon we drove to The Meadows and upon arrival we met a short man in jeans who introduced himself as Pat Melody, the founder of the center. He opened the institution to treat his fellow veterans addicted to alcohol and drugs.

He asked about my working experience and when he heard I was a priest, a psychologist, a university professor and therapist for sex offenders on parole in New Brunswick he said I undoubtedly met the prerequisites because they were planning on opening an institute for sex offender clergymen. It was a sure shot; a dream and I was understandably excited. Rina told me I shouldn't get too excited and count my chickens before they hatch. She was absolutely correct because when Pat tested the market with bishops and ecclesiastics, he hit the preverbal brick wall and up went my dream in a puff of smoke.

I liked Pat's idea of a program for sex offender clergymen as the need is definitely there but the bishops and the churches are not, they are on the defensive.

We bought a house with two apartments in Wickenburg. It sat on a 2 1/2-acre lot and Rina turned it into a Bed and Breakfast establishment with five bedrooms. It was a perfect set-up for a small treatment center. I envisaged a five-week intensive relapse prevention program using the Pathways Model for sex offender clergymen. *The Pathways Model identifies five etiological pathways, pathways concerned with the causes and origins of diseases; each path with primary psychological deficits that interact to create a vulnerability to sexual offending behavior.* I decided to go ahead with the project and mailed a letter with brochures to 359 Anglican, Roman Catholic and Episcopalian bishops in Canada and U.S.A.

I hit the same wall as did Pat Melody. I received only sixteen replies and not one recognized the need of such a program claiming they didn't have a problem. The only bishop who interfaced with me was the Roman Catholic bishop of Arizona who sent two priests to get more information. They were polite but aloof and uninterested. It appeared I wasn't trustworthy because I broke my promise of celibacy. That was the end of my program. The inner sanctum of the Church cannot be breached.

Dr. Leo R. Theriault
701 South Saguaro Drive
PO Box 20370
Wickenburg, AZ 85358
(520) 684-1177 fax (520) 684-1255

Dear Bishop................:
Enclosed please find brochures describing who I am and what I do. I've also enclosed my resume and a treatment program for sex offender clergymen.

I took an early retirement from Universite de Moncton, Canada, last year and moved to Arizona for my wife's arthritis. We found this peaceful parcel of land in the "cowboy town" of Wickenburg, famous for its upside down river. When I saw this property I knew it was an ideal spot for an intensive therapy retreat. I do not want to retire completely and I intend to work as long as I may.

In June 1998, I will celebrate my 40th anniversary of ordination to priesthood. Being a priest at heart, I value the welfare of priests and clergymen. I am known as a good psychologist and my layout could be very efficient for priests going through rough times. I would enjoy very much being able to apply my energy to aid healing amongst churches and contribute to the betterment of the mystical body of Christ.

Although the retreat is open to any problems, including addiction, one very specific form of treatment that I want to bring to your attention is the treatment of pedophiles or sex offenders. In 1967, my first client during my practicum in in clinical psychology was a pedophile priest. From 1991, til (sic) my move, I was on contract with Correctional Services Canada, to treat sex offenders on parole. I was also in charge of three programs for the treatment of French sex offenders in the prison system of New Brunswick, Canada. The 14 week programs used the Relapse Prevention Model which is the favored and most efficient treatment model by Correctional Services Canada. The therapy sessions were given two afternoons a week for 14 weeks. The parallel treatment program can very well be given five days a week for four weeks. The program description has been enclosed in this letter.

Slight modification of this program to four weeks, presented the practicality of such a program for clergymen sex offenders:

1. *Time factor:* one month instead of four

2. *Anonymity:* the clergyman goes on a vacation or retreat to Arizona for a month

3. *Number of participants:* no more than five at a time

4. *Homogeneity of the group:* all clergymen

5. *Location:* a peacefulness of the desert is an asset

6. *Christian orientation* of the program

It is required by Arizona law that notification be made to the local law enforcement agency of presence of *convicted* child molesters. *Convicted* sex offenders are not allowed to cross the U.S./Canadian border either, therefore I have the availability to present this program in New Brunswick, Canada for Canadian *convicted* sex offenders. I am still a registered psychologist and have maintained my coverage of professional liability insurance there.

I know resources for the treatment of clergy sex offenders are very limited. This undertaking will help protect Christ's flock through me and you. I would appreciate receiving your reactions to this program outline and welcome you to come and visit. I also am receptive to any suggestions you may have to enhance this programs practicality for clergy.

Sincerely in Christ,
Leo R. Theriault, Psy.D.

Copy of promotional brochures follow in the appendix, page 135.

Chapter XXI

ON THE HIT LIST

W hile I was counseling juvenile delinquents the Arizona Director of Adult Probation asked me to give a Relapse Prevention Program for ten of her sex offenders on probation. Lies, secrecy, shame, compulsivity, insecurity, loneliness, and infidelity can all be side effects of sexual addiction. The net result is often a withdrawal from others and from healthy habits and behaviors. Alcoholic Anonymous has a warning sign for adherents to be especially careful when they are hungry, angry, lonely, or tired; H*A*L*T. Counseling can often retard the negative behavior and can address any underlying issues that contributed to the behavior in the first place – but there isn't a cure. The best our profession can do is to develop, implement and follow through with a relapse prevention program.

We start with disclosure. The offender must reveal the names of his or her victims, their age, the way they were groomed or seduced, and the consequences of the abuse on the victims. An individual relapse prevention plan is then developed. As an example, if the victims are between the ages of five and ten years old the perpetrator must be segregated from this age group. The first step in the relapse prevention plan is to assure the culprit is never alone with minors. The symptom is like an allergy. If you are allergic to roses you don't work in a rose garden. If you are an alcoholic you don't work in a bar. A child molester will succumb to his or her weakness or perversion when alone with a child. It was a thirteen-week program of two only two- hour sessions per week for a total of fifty-two of group counseling for adult offenders. Individual counseling was also available. There were ten in my group that included a retired policeman, a Presbyterian minister and a businessman.

One attendee was the most despicable antisocial person I ever had the misfortune to encounter. He arrived at the first meeting with long grey hair and beard, a padded bra, bare feet, and wearing a petticoat; an actual lady's underskirt. He was fifty-five years of age. All in attendance were shocked with his appearance and demeanor and some didn't want to continue with him in the group. I told them they had a choice of either going back to prison or staying and ignoring him. Interestingly this cretin lived in the desert where Tim McVey lived when he bombed the Federal Building in Oklahoma.

The first month went well as could be expected from such an assembly; a lot of denial – being framed, victims being liars, the investigation being rigged, and so on. Gradually they started disclosing the truth and their anxieties.

Our desert denizen was different. His anger was palpable. He venomously voiced the opinion all police and probation officers should be killed. He was scurrilous to all authority. He attempted to shock everyone and was surprised and shaken when he was ignored by everyone. Nevertheless, he never missed one session and was never late. He never disclosed nor worked on a relapse prevention plan and after a month he asked me for individual counseling.

He trusted no one. He never had a friend because he never let anyone get close to him. The closest he got to anyone was the adolescent he was found guilty of sexually molesting. He was always protecting himself from a supposed hostile environment. He was so unfriendly he assured the environment would remain hostile. He could not allow himself to be happy. He was always angry. The individual counseling partly relieved his anger, but he was not ready to deal with the possible root cause of his problem – he had a very abusive childhood.

On week twelve of the program when each group member was asked what they learned from the program all were surprised when he responded he had never had a moment of happiness in his entire life but thanks to my individual counseling he could see a little light at the end of the tunnel. Someday perhaps he could have a few moments of happiness. He continued he learned that policemen and probation officers were human beings just like him. He had never seen it like that before.

He confided we in positions of power had been on his hit list, the receiving end of a gun – the ex-police officer, the Director of Adult Probation, the parole officer, and me. After just 12 weeks of personal counseling we were off the list and were "free" men. The program had apparently worked. We were understandably delighted with his change in attitude, but we were in for another surprise.

The following morning, our 13th week and final day of counseling, he had to go to register as a sex offender at the Motor Vehicle office and have his offence placed on his driver's license. He went but threw a tantrum and left without registering. That evening he arrived for his 25th session as if nothing had happened. His probation officer told him he had no choice but to take him back to jail upon which he stormed out leaving behind, "You know where I live."

The Director of Adult Probation was not pleased that our misfit had already left. She then decided she and his probation officer would assemble the police and arrest him, in the desert if necessary. I told her he would not be taken alive. He would take his own life, provoke suicide by cop, or shoot his way clear. Each scenario was exceedingly abhorrent. I recommended they wait until morning, daylight, before they attempted anything. I also recommended they leave the task solely to the police. They disregarded both my recommendations; damn the torpedoes, full steam ahead.

I terminated our session and told everyone to go directly home and to be very careful, especially while leaving the building. We had no idea what he might do. The law enforcement cadre went to his trailer in the desert, but it was vacant. In searching his premises, they found a fully loaded sub-machine gun under his pillow, a fully loaded rifle in the corner and a variety of pornographic videos. They returned to town at about two a.m. and received a call from his trailer park neighbor claiming she heard gun shots from the vicinity of his digs. The squad went back to his quarters and found our misbegotten dead; he had shot himself.

I did not sleep well that night not knowing what to expect and fearing the worse. In the morning I went nervously to the Probation Office. The probation officer was there and he seemed to be every bit as anxious as I. He explained the events of early morning and I was crestfallen, but relieved no one else was hurt. Another probation officer overhearing our conversation asked if, due to the suicide, I thought the program was a success or failure. I replied as tragic as the result may be no one else was hurt. I continued that our poor unfortunate had earlier threatened us all, plus any policeman in range, yet he didn't shoot anyone but himself. I emphasized that a sub-machine gun was for hunting man and not animals, yet he hunted no one. I told him yes, if the program changed his mind about killing his fellow man, I would consider the program a success.

I was never contacted by the police or the authorities of Correctional Services about this suicide.

The probation officer and his wife were so traumatized by the event that he quit and returned to his home state in search of another kind of social service position. No more correctional services for them.

Being on a hit list is not a bowl of cherries.

Chapter XXII

PEDOPHILIA AND THE CHURCH

For decades pedophilia has been a major problem in the Catholic Church. Of course, it was always problematic, but in relatively recent years it seems to have become an epidemic; overt with public outcry and publicity. The Second Vatican Council's directives might have given parishioners the courage to come forward and even question the authority of the once omnipotent priest. Priest celibacy is purported to be the root cause of pedophilia, but I feel differently. A priest is not a pedophile because he is celibate, but a pedophile can become a priest. A pedophile looks for a position of authority over his victims, and the clergy is an excellent position of authority for a pedophile as are many other positions of power such as judges, lawyers, coaches, teachers, parents, actors, the famous, et al. Because of the calling of and the dedication to the church, the clergy at one time was the last place one would expect to find sexual aberrancy.

A pedophile priest is not necessarily authoritarian, but some are sexually immature and seem to be stuck at puberty level of mental development; behaving as boys at this level of maturity. We call it development freeze. It is as if their emotional past has stopped at puberty or adolescent level. They get along well with minors because they themselves are minors in adult bodies. They enjoy camping with minors and will sexually abuse them if and when the opportunity arises. They enjoy fishing trips or other excursions with one or a few minors.

Mothers, insecure with teaching sex to their teenage children, often ask the parish priest to educate their boy or girl about sexuality. It is like giving free reign to a pedophile.

Ministry is supposed to be a helping profession and not an abusing vocation, or avocation as the case may be. Clearly it is not always the case. Priesthood can be a good hiding place, a good sanctuary, for a pedophile. The good shepherd loves his sheep and will risk his life to protect his flock. The wolf loves lamb chops. When the wolf finishes devouring a sheep, the sheep has been destroyed. A priest is expected to be a good shepherd, not a wolf. The priest is expected to protect his congregate and not destroy any part thereof, especially a child.

When I was ordained, I had no idea the problem was so rife but in later years my work as a psychologist put me in direct contact with the victims. Later yet my contract with parole boards put me in direct contact with offenders. During my family counseling I interacted with the spouses and children of incest offenders. I do not pretend to be an expert in the field of pedophilia and incest, but I have been considered as such by the courts of the land.

The case in 1967 of Pam and Archbishop Robichaud was a shocking wake-up call for me. Saving Pam from a death sentence was gratifying but the Archbishop's cover-up of the priest who raped her was beyond understanding. I was further confused by Bishop Lacroix, whom I highly respected, allowing a pedophile priest be transferred to the position of school chaplain in the diocese of Québec after knowing full well his history of pedophilia.

Keeping my own company, I asked how could a good shepherd allow the wolf devour his lambs? How and why could they look the other way? Were they themselves pedophiles? This is a question that has forever haunted me because I too had looked the other way. In 2018, fifty years hence, I may have some partial answers but condoning those bishops who did not and do not protect their flock is not in my psyche.

We are amazed and dismayed by the frequency of sexual abuse by people in authority; engagements are coming to light with untold regularity. Mass and social media are exposing the sins that were in the dark for centuries. With this "new" enlightenment comes the knowledge of sexual ignorance, false beliefs and false teachings. Christian dogma once taught humans were composed of two entities, the body and the soul. The body came from the devil and the soul from God. This duality of body and soul obviously opened the door for misinterpretation, manipulation and misuse. If the body comes from the devil, then all bodily pleasure is sinful. It is a sin to enjoy food. It is a sin to enjoy sex. Sexuality is spiritually only for reproduction therefore any form of sexual pleasure is a sin.

A past associate, Father Lacouture, went as far as saying smoking was as sinful as fornication. Some priests jokingly said if they had a choice, they would quit smoking. Some religious orders had the "discipline" of self-flagellation to punish themselves for sins of the flesh. The confessional was a swinging door to transgression; sin, "sin no more my son," sin, "say 100 Hail Mary's," sin, ad infinitum. The notion of sexual pleasure coming from the devil opened the door to sexual repression as well as sexual deviance with all the bad consequences therein.

Pedophilia is not exclusive to celibate catholic priests. All religious denominations possibly and probably have their share of pedophile clergymen. After all, they're in positions of authority.

Emory University psychiatrist Dr. Gene Abel reported men who molested boys had an astonishing average of 150 victims and male offenders who abused girls had an average of 52. An Arizona priest arrested for pedophilia kept a list of his victim's names and it exceeded 400; he even evaluated their sexual performance on a scale of one to ten.

When pedophiles are queried as to why many of their victims don't report their offence their decided answer is often, "We know how to spot and choose the ones who won't talk." Shame and embarrassment follow suit.

A school principal in a rural area of New Brunswick was arrested for sexually abusing students over decades and not one victim had come forth. Nor did the bystanders – the school council, the clergy, the parents, fellow students – no one.

Jesus had good reason to compare society to a flock of sheep. Sheep are defenseless whereas the predator, the wolf, creates panic. The sheep run hither and yon and eventually bunch together each trying to reach the center for maximum security. The wolf circles the flock, menacing them until one of them panics, flees the flock and becomes the wolf's dinner. So often the lamb is caught because of their inability to hide or keep up with the flock. Amazingly, while the wolf is devouring its victim, other sheep return to their normal activity, grazing, and some even go to smell the victim while the wolf is still eating. Danger has past until the wolf is again hungry. A good shepherd protects his flock while the hired hand watches.

Richard Sipe, a former Benedictine monk-priest of 18 years and a sociologist, is the author of six books about Catholicism and the sexual abuses arising from the Catholic Church's requirements of celibacy. In his book *Sex, Priest and Power* he reports attending a conference of US bishops whereby a reporter asked why their fellow bishops tolerated pedophilia priests within their diocese. One bishop responded, "Maybe because they themselves are pedophiles." The reporter couldn't believe his ears so repeated his question and got the same response. It begs the question as to who would dare report a bishop. The victim is powerless. What child, or parent, would call a priest, let alone a bishop, a liar? Who will take the word of a minor against the word of an ecclesiast? The victims live with their painful secret that will damage their entire life. The onlookers and passersby shrug and proceed with their personal lives.

Victims report feeling empty, dead inside and have very poor self-esteem. Some feel dirty and shower two or three times a day. Some feel confused because they are taught extramarital sex is forbidden, is a sin, yet a priest, a judge or a relative is having sex with them. Some feel both fear and guilt if the predator threatens them with hell damnation or presages their mother or grandmother will die if the secret comes out – and it will be their entire fault. Some develop sexual frigidity while others promiscuity. Some will reject having children fearing a repeat of their own existence or fear their offspring will become abusers. Some become substance abusers to kill the mental anguish. Some will enact what they feel is expected; debauchery. In extreme cases some will surrender life and commit suicide.

Over a two-year period headlines in Canadian "screamed":

4 New Brunswick priests caught in Sexual abuse allegations – October 7, 2016

5 Lawsuits in three months – October 24, 2016

2 new lawsuits filed against ex-priest and Moncton archbishop – July 27, 2017

Convicted Moncton ex-priest will face preliminary inquiry on new sex charge next month – Aug 9th, 2017

56 lawsuits against Catholic Church that allege sexual abuse are before N.B. courts – Nov.15, 2017

I crossed paths with most of the accused, but had a particular interest in one Father Rino Deschenes, the same Deschenes outlined in chapter VIII. In August of 2016 two lawsuits were filed against Deschenes and the Edmundston Diocese, alleging he repeatedly abused two young boys, aged between nine and 13, when he was a priest in Riviere-Verte Church. According to the lawsuit, Deschenes admitted to the allegations in letters to the victims. In October 2016 Deschenes was currently in prison, after pleading guilty in 2015 to five sex-related charges, including indecency and sodomy. He was sentenced to seven and a half years in prison.

Sylvia MacEachern, a grandmother of 11 residing in Ottawa, Canada, has an unshakable devotion to the Catholic faith matched only by her tireless pursuit of clergy members accused of sex crimes. For years she has been a familiar face at trials and investigations into church scandals and consequently has amassed a huge collection of files, transcripts and other documents. With this compilation in 2010 she launched a Word-Press-based blog and database called *Sylvia's Site*.

The website has showcased an ever-expanding rogues' gallery of Catholic Church abusers or suspects. The alphabetical catalogue includes clergy members who were charged and convicted for their crimes, but also those who have successfully appealed, who reached settlements with their alleged victims, or have simply been named in investigations. At printing, the index contains 350 people in the "accused" section only – all and only Canadian!

Sylvia says she has been shocked by the "abysmal" way the diocese treated the victims and disgusted by the level of denial among parishioners even after a priest pleaded guilty.

As earlier reported, when René Lévesque said, "Québec needs fewer steeples and more factory chimneys" he sent a shock wave throughout the entire Catholic populace of the province. As a young priest I was stunned by this provocation. The church was the house of God and also the rallying place for the community. But René Lévesque was right.

Church steeples were the GPS, global positioning system, of the day. You could barely leave one town or village when you could see the looming spire of the next settlement. Industrialization meant more chimneys and they were becoming the new referral point of orientation. The Church was even losing out in global direction; literally and not figuratively. René Lévesque used the metaphor to say it was time to proceed and break with tradition. But tradition was also the Church. Tradition was the flywheel by which society maintained stability. It could also, however, be the pothole of society by blocking progress. It was time for social order to fill the holes.

René Lévesque's proclamation about steeples and chimneys has become a reality.

Many churches closed and many more united into one parish. I have mixed feelings when I see such beautiful churches in the course of decay. I admire their beauty and the faith of the parishioners who had the talent and desire to build these magnificent houses of God. Many could ill afford such indulgence, but their faith was stronger than their earthly needs. I often wonder whether the church was built in honor of God or for the vanity of the bishop and/or the parish priest.

I then recall Mathew 24:2 when Jesus was at the Temple of Jerusalem with his disciples who were admiring the Temple's magnificence. Jesus said unto them, "See ye not all these things? Verily I say unto you, there shall not be left here one stone upon another that shall not be thrown down." Incredulity cannot define their emotions. How could such a magnificent house of God be destroyed? God could never allow his house to be destroyed.

Once again, I recall the Book of Mathew (21:13): And Jesus said, "It is written, My house shall be called the house of prayer; but ye have made it a den of thieves." He threw the dealers out of the Temple using a whip and upsetting their business tables. A church is a building that can be used to pray to God and to praise God or it can be used for financial benefits for a few in the name of God. Things have not changed since the time of Christ. It happened at the time of Jesus, it is happening today, and most likely will continue to happen in the future. Many, like me, feel closer to God and prefer praying in a chapel or a poor mission than in an opulent cathedral or church.

Too often in my adopted country Mexico I see poor communities with magnificent churches gilded with gold and I have to question whether they were built for God or the conscience of gold mining companies, or the bribes of the gold barons. The poor are still poor and the gold mines are long gone. The raising of a church is not the will of God but too often a decision of mortals for greed or power rather than for faith. The Church of God is for the people of God, not the buildings of God.

The transition from spire to stack was easy to forecast but bishopric authority felt secure with the status quo and didn't want to rock the boat. They led from behind and did not dare take the lead to greener pastures.

There were, of course, exceptions. Archbishop Vienneau of the archdiocese of Moncton, New Brunswick, dared take the lead. He told the victims of pedophilic priests, "I am on your side. It is not your fault. It is the fault of priests who behaved and behave like wolves. They aren't the shepherds they are supposed to be but are wolves in sheep clothing. I will do my best to alleviate your pain." He took the lead at the risk of bankrupting his diocese. He followed the teachings of Jesus and placed his person in peril. He was a leader and not a follower. He was a shepherd.

In 2012 Vienneau initiated a Reconciliation Process (the Sacrament of Penance and Reconciliation is one of the seven sacraments of the Catholic Church in which the faithful obtain absolution for the sins committed against God and neighbors and are reconciled with the community of the Church) overseen independently by retired Supreme Court Justice, the Honorable Michel Bastarache. Justice Bastarache was to administer the settlement of class-action sexual harassment lawsuits by acting as an independent assessor of the claims to be submitted. Justice Bastarache was a puisne justice on the Supreme Court of Canada from 1997 through 2008. Unlike the United States, Supreme Court justices are not appointed for life, but may sit on the bench until the mandatory retirement age of 75. Tenure has ranged from 101 days to 37 years. Bastarache was designated the "sole and independent decision maker" for the claims process.

The sexes offended were to be represented by his or her independent lawyer and the Church was represented by a so-called Devil's advocate. The Devil's advocate of the Church, originally established in 1587, was a canon lawyer appointed by Church authorities to argue against the canonization of a candidate. It was this person's job to take a skeptical view of the candidate's character, to look for holes in the evidence, to argue that any miracles attributed to the candidate were fraudulent, and so on. Pope John Paul II reduced the power and changed the role of the office in 1983.

The reconciliation process was meant to provide compensation to victims and show the Church took its role seriously; their primary purpose was to effect reconciliation and to seek forgiveness of those who were sinned against.

Justice Bastarache was reputed as being speedy and fair and provided a dignified environment to bring forth the victims' experiences. No group, be they churches, police forces, teachers, scout leaders, charitable foundations or especially the clergy knew just how seriously these types of abuses harmed victims. The public in general did not recognize the damages caused by sexual abuse.

Bishop Vienneau, recognizing the scourge of such abuse and in full recognition of its evil, established a heightened program of abuse prevention and protocols to dissuade abusers. All priests, including the bishop, diocesan and parish employees, and all volunteers with children or vulnerable people had to be cleared by the police.

The immensity, tragedy and callousness of the judgments were far reaching. The audacity and depravity of the priests is wordless; the pain and suffering of the victims and their families horrific. The concealed fallout is the prevalent closing of parish churches. The denial and disavowal by the bishoprics, indeed the papacy, was deemed disingenuous by many parishioners leaving many pews empty. Payment of the deserved but substantial compensations to the victims has bankrupt many parishes. Many churches that have survived keep two sets of ledgers, one for the diocese and a hidden one for their own administration and physical upkeep; physical survival.

The Christian Daily of November 2017 reported: The Catholic Church in Canada could be driven to bankruptcy because of the numerous ongoing sex abuse lawsuits against priests which could easily cost millions of dollars, according to a local archbishop.

Speaking to the Canadian Broadcasting Corporation News in an interview, Archbishop Vienneau said their diocese previously had money "but doesn't anymore." A recent report by the CBC outlined the financial repercussions of the sex abuse cases on the Catholic Church in New Brunswick. The archdiocese of Moncton shelled out $10.6 million Canadian dollars for the 109 alleged abuse victims from 2012 to 2014, while Bathurst had to pay $5.5 million to 90 alleged victims.

"And to say that the bankruptcy would fix things is, I think, quite improbable. Because there are no assets left except the churches themselves. And I don't know who would want to buy a church," CBC quoted Michel Bastarache.

Chapter XXIII

SLINGS AND ARROWS

I have always loved teaching and preaching and have often been told my homilies convey a good message and are "down to earth"; in farmers language I bring the hay to the horses. I have often been told children enjoy my sermons which is an anomaly to convention. I usually get positive feedback even when I address sensitive topics. A case in point, mentioned earlier, was when I addressed the topic of a Christian approach to sexuality at l'Ecole de la Foi and received a standing ovation from the lay people in attendance. The bishop gave me laudation but one month later I was ousted from l'Ecole de la Foi by Father Lachace and the bishop looked the other way. I received two more standing ovations after two sermons in Arizona, one on love and one on Christian sexuality. As English is my second language, I was particularly pleased to receive such ovations.

Not long after I joined the Anglican Church in 1995 I was supplying for the priest of Centerville, Arizona and the gospel for the day was the multiplication of the loaves. The miracle goes against the Law of Nature, so I presented an analogy. I explained how I was sharing knowledge with them, each would leave more enriched no matter the size of the congregation, and I would leave without losing anything. I continued the same applied to a family. A child would not be loved only one third if he or she was of a family with three children. The more love one shared the more one had to share. After the service a mother told me her ten year old boy didn't want to attend church that morning but after my sermon he was glad he came. He said he understood my message. That felt good to hear, but such is not always the case.

It is a given if you attack pedophilia you had better be ready to be attacked viciously in return. As mentioned earlier, it occurred with the Group of Seven during my childhood. Early backers are usually weak of commitment. I was disappointment on two occasions when I addressed pedophilia from the pulpit and called them perverts. The first was in 1996 and the last was in 2014. The latter happened to be my last sermon. Both had a polarizing effect on the congregation. In 1996 I asked the senior warden to check the reaction of the congregation and the results were: university graduates were most favorable, the majority favorable and a small group were astonished. As expected, those surprised were the most vociferous.

The following emails attests to the dynamics of the congregation. On a Sunday in April, 2014 I gave a sermon in St. Andrew's Anglican Church in the vicinity of Lake Chapala, México. Lake Chapala is about 70 kilometers (40 Miles) south of Guadalajara.

Email number one was the most contemptible attack on me I have encountered in 60 years in the priesthood.

> Sermon 27 April 2014
> To Leo, Winston (Parish Priest), Members of the Personnel Committee and the Vestry of St. Andrew's Anglican Church:
>
> I am writing to you because I love the music ministry I do at St. Andrew's and also because I care deeply about the congregation and their spiritual growth through the Word and sacrament. Today was the third time I have had to witness a disgusting and inappropriate sermon from the Rev. Dr. Leo: child abuse, pedophilia, cutting of their ding-a-lings. In other words: non-gospel topic, judgmental and violence. I feel as a member of the congregation and as the minister of music I cannot tolerate this anymore. I was embarrassed to be a member of this congregation today. I was embarrassed for the members and many visitors. I would never come back to a church where I heard "preaching" like that. And on children's Sunday? The last time this happened I expressed to the Sr. Warden and Rector I would not play nor direct the choir if he preached on these topics again. He has. Enough. In other words, if the Rev. Dr. Leo is asked to preach again I will call in sick - because that is what his sermons do to me.
>
> Minister of Music
> St. Andrew's Anglican Church

Email number two came from a member of the choir.

> Subject: Children's Sunday
> To: Leo
>
> I have been thinking about how to address much of the subject matter in Sunday's sermon on one of the happiest Sundays (or should be) in our Christian heritage. I do know most of you, and will probably meet all of you at some time during our church services. I did not realize that last Sunday was to be Children's Sunday because in my church in New England we celebrated in June. To

see all of those beautiful, excited, proud and happy children taking part in our services was so wonderful and the work that Barbara and Norinne have contributed to the Sunday school is fantastic. Kudos to them both.

The sermon delivered by Leo was horrific, embarrassing, shameful and totally tasteless. It had absolutely nothing to do with celebrating children and their very special place in our hearts and the world. There are many atrocities throughout the world occurring every second of the day, but Children's Sunday should not be a time to discuss pedophilia and the most egregious of all remarks - the cutting off of a ding-a-ling? I could not believe that Leo said that, nor could I believe that I actually heard that reference during a sermon at church at St. Andrews in Ajijic. There is no more that I can say about how I felt Sunday, but all of you are part of the workings of St. Andrew's. I hope you take the proper steps to make sure that the pulpit is held in high esteem, and that Leo not be allowed to take part in another sermon. I understand that this is not the first time there has been this type of behavior.

Thank you for taking the time to read this and I hope all of you will respond to the behavior that was presented appropriately.

A Concerned Parishioner

Email number three came from a member of the vestry.
[Note: After the mass she told me my sermon was excellent and that I should preach on that topic every time I could. After Tim's critique she seems to have changed her mind.]

Sermon 27 April, 2014
Tim:

Your email is thought provoking. I listened to the sermon and appreciated that Fr. Leo addressed the issue of the Sunday school kids. That meant a lot to me as there are a number of folks in the church who "don't want the children to touch me." "These children should not be in church" and on and on. I watched the faces of those folks and they looked uncomfortable. That, I appreciated. I heard the rest of the sermon, but did not give it much thought. Having said that, you are right, he went too far. All in all, unfortunate.

Thank you for speaking up and straightening me out!

If you preach to a congregation of 100 or more people, odds are there are more than one victim of sexual child abuse and the possibility of one or more abusers in attendance. You do not know how they will react. This

Congregationalist told me that my sermon was long overdue and told me to preach on that topic every chance I get, but as soon as I was attacked by the Minister of Music she thanked him for straightening her out. My sermon was excellent as long as it was not attacked, but as soon as I was attacked she sided with the attacker, which is very typical of victims. It is called the Stockholm syndrome whereby the attacker is considered as a savior. The Stockholm syndrome is a condition that causes hostages to develop a psychological alliance with their captors as a survival strategy during captivity. These alliances, resulting from a bond formed between captor and captives during intimate time spent together, are generally considered irrational in light of the danger or risk endured by the victims. Patty Hearst with the Symbionese Liberation Army is a case in point.

It could also be called the Apostle Peter Syndrome. When the going got rough, he denied knowing Jesus to protect himself, even if he had promised that he would die to protect Jesus. If you attack a wolf pedophile you had better be prepared to be alone; your supporters may be far behind you. They mind their own business and do not want to get involved but you still must do your job as a good shepherd. Silence is letting the abuser get away with and deserting the victims.

Monsignor Conway, Rector of the Cathedral of Edmundston for over 50 years, was respected by his parishioners and fellow priests. When a priest was appointed Rector of a parish for the first time he would be told, "If you never have problems with the choir or the graveyard, you will be a happy priest." He was referring to the divisiveness of both entities; the choir being the center of rumors, in-fighting and power; the necropolis separating the community through the last rites (or lack thereof), mixed marriages, or even the care or neglect of the cemetery itself. He was right.

My last sermon was attacked by the Minister of Music followed by a few who thought they were in control of the parish. The Minister of Music was dictating who could and who could not preach as well as the topic of the sermon. The priest's priority is to preach the Gospel of Jesus and not the gospel according to a few elitists. After 60 years of ordination to priesthood, my last sermon did not receive a standing ovation. It was not the swan song I expected or desired.

Email number four came from another member of the vestry.

Hi Leo,

We are travelling and just got caught up with the flap about your sermon. IGNORE them! I told you on the way out the door that it was a good sermon and I heard that from a few people as I made my way from the front of the Church to the back. You were happy that it was short and I said yes, 12 minutes. So again ignore the few. You can't please everyone but you please my wife and me.

Take care and see you when we get back on the 11th. You certainly have our support.

Supportive Couple

Email number five was my response to the Choir manager.

Sermon 27 April, 2014
Tim,

After the service on April 27th (children's Sunday) I received very positive feedback from the congregation like, 'excellent sermon, very gospel, very good application of the gospel, long overdue, please continue every chance you get'.

Then I received your email telling me that my sermon was "non-gospel topic, judgmental and violent." I disagree with you. My sermon was very gospel. I followed very closely two texts of the gospel. The first text Mark 10: 13-16 deals with the disciples pushing away children and Jesus being INDIGNANT for their rejection. I applied it to Sunday school at St. Andrews. I gave my full support to the volunteers, without attacking those who resent the presence of those children in the church. Tim, who is non-gospel? I or those who do not accept the children in the church? In Mark 10: 13-16. The second text is Matthew 18: 1-10. Who is greatest in Heaven? Jesus called a child and said "those who are childlike." Then Jesus goes on to say that anyone causing a child's downfall. It would be better for him to have a milestone tied to his neck. When we know that a pedophile will abuse an average of 365 children in their lifetime. It is very serious. What is non-gospel in applying Jesus' milestone to them? Then Jesus goes further saying, "If your hand or your foot causes your downfall cut it off." Then I added, "What would Jesus say to a pedophile? Would he tell him to cut his ding-a-ling?" Maybe ding-a-ling was not the appropriate word. I would appreciate you telling me what is the appropriate word to call the part of the body used by the pedophile to abuse his victim the child. The violent and judgmental words off cutting off and millstone tied to the neck are the words of Jesus, not mine.

Your comments of my sermon being non-gospel, violence and judgmental and very rude and unfair.

I was ordained to priesthood 56 years ago. As priest we are

called to be good shepherds. That is to LEAD the flock to the green pasture of the Gospel and also to PROTECT it from the destructive wolves. Do you agree that pedophiles are wolves feeding on the lamb? Do you agree that a bishop who covers up for pedophile priests is a shepherd letting the wolf in the flock to devour the lamb instead of risking his life to protect the sheep? I personally know a few adolescents who committed suicide after being molested by pedophiles. I also personally know many attempted suicides due to pedophilia. How many victims of pedophilia go through life feeling like "dirt," "piece of shit," "dead inside," "taking shower after shower and still feeling dirty." "Why do I destroy those I love"? Tim, those are real people, not the product of my imagination. I called pedophiles "perverts" and perverts they are. The milestone is waiting for them unless they REPENT, which means BREAKING AWAY WITH THEIR PERVERT BEHAVIOUR. That is what Jesus meant when he used the analogy of "cutting off and throwing away." The covering up for pedophiles has left wolf pedophilia feed freely on the nice fat lamb and become a Monster Cancer that is killing the Church. I WILL NOT SHY AWAY FROM PROTECTING THE SHEEP FROM THE WOLF AND I INTEND TO CONTINUE ATTACKING THE WOLF as a good shepherd should do.

On April 27th I was happy to supply for Fr. Winston to permit him to be at his mother's side for her last moments on earth. I surely was not expecting my sermon to create such a polarizing effect in the parish. The last thing I wanted to do was to disturb Fr. Winston in this time of grief and worry about Mary's surgery. But it did not seem to bother some members of the Congregation. I did not know that you had told Fr. Winston and the Sr. Warden that you did not want me to preach anymore at St. Andrews. They never told me and they did not have to. Because it is not the responsibility of the Master of Music to decide who can preach or cannot preach and to decide the topic of the sermon.

I have been debating if your rudeness deserved a reply or if I should just let go since I am a retired member of the Congregation and available to supply if needed. Since I witnessed your rudeness towards other members of the Congregation, one I never saw again at church. When I saw your lack of consideration towards Fr. Winston during his time of grief. Your complaint could have waited after his return. There was absolutely no emergency. That was very rude on your part. But I suppose you were angry because you had told him that you did not want me to preach anymore and here I was. He did not follow your command. But remember he is not a member of the choir to follow your command. He is the Rector. He and the Sr. Warden are not your employees as far as I know.

Now I have a problem. On June 29th, I will be celebrating 56 years of ordination to priesthood. I intended to ask Fr. Winston to preach on that Sunday. But due to the major storm in a glass of water that we just lived through, I will just forget about it. I will talk to Fr. Winston when he comes back and let him finish his leave of absence in peace.

Tim, you are an outstanding choirmaster. If there is ever an opening in Heaven for a Choirmaster-in-chief, I will gladly support you. But do not ask me to support you as a Good Shepherd-in-chief.

I will continue to attend at St. Andrews. I will be available to supply if needed as long as my health permits. And I will continue enjoying Fr. Winston's sermons as well the music and choir.

Christianly yours
Fr. Leo

Subscript: The children were having Sunday school lessons while I was preaching and did not hear my sermon. I never suspected my sermon would cause such consternation; mind you, from only a very few. Nonetheless, if you attack pedophilia from the pulpit you must expect retaliations. It is a very sensitive topic about a very secretive world that touches the victims as well as the offenders. Both are uncomfortable thinking about it let alone talk about it. Victims sense they are alone with such a problem so when it is openly aired they feel they are being directly addressed. The offender feels extreme distress fearing exposure and his fears turns to anger. Father Joe Paul Levesque, who baptized me, became extremely angry when he was exposed and attacked his accusers. They were the Seven Deadly Sinners.

In the summer of 2020, Leo died in his hometown of Drummond, New Brunswick, Canada at the age of 86. He suffered for 15 years of the debilitating disease of Parkinson's.

Epilogue

MOLESTER STATISTICS

The following statements might be considered in a subjective vein:

The serial killer has the same personality characteristics as the sex offender against children.
– Dr. Mace Knapp, Nevada State Prison Psychologist

There are 400,000 registered sex offenders in the United States, and an estimated 80 to 100,000 of them are missing. They're supposed to be registered, but we don't know where they are and we don't know where they're living.
– Ernie Allen, President of the National Center for Missing and Exploited Children

The most serious and chronic offenders often show signs of antisocial behavior as early as preschool years.
– American Psychiatric Association, 1994

Dr. Gene Abel, an American psychiatrist and couple's counselor who also works with men and boys suspected of sexual deviancy, estimates that between 1% and 5% of our population molest children.
– CNN Specials Transcript #454-Thieves of Childhood

Nearly all the offenders in sexual assaults reported to law enforcement were male (96%).
– Sexual Assault of Young Children as Reported to Law Enforcement, 7/00, NCJ 182990, U.S. Department of Justice

Overall, 23% of sexual assault offenders were under the age of 18 and 77% were adults.
– Sexual Assault of Young Children as reported to Law Enforcement, 7/00, NCJ 182990, U.S. Department of Justice

40% of the victims under age six were themselves juveniles. A similar proportion (39%) of offenders of victims six through 11 were

also juveniles. For older juvenile victims, the proportion of juvenile offenders dropped to 27%.
– Sexual Assault of Young Children as reported to Law Enforcement, 7/00, NCJ 182990, U.S. Department of Justice

Adults were the offenders in 60% of the sexual assaults of youth under age 12. Rarely were the offenders of young victims strangers. Strangers were the offender in just 3% of sexual assaults against victims under age six and 5% of the sexual assault of victimizations of youth ages six through 11.
– Sexual Assault of Young Children as reported to Law Enforcement, 7/00, NCJ 182990, U.S. Department of Justice

One in five offenders serving time in a state prison reported having victimized a child.
– BJS Survey of State Prison Inmates, 1991.

2/3 of all prisoners convicted of rape or sexual assault had committed their crime against a child.
– Bureau of Justice Statistics (BJS) Survey of State Prison Inmates, 1991

Acquaintance perpetrators are the most common abusers, constituting approximately 70-90% of all reported perpetrators.
– Simon David Finkelhor, American sociologist known for his research into child sexual abuse

89% of sexual child cases involve persons known to the child, such as a caretaker of family acquaintance.
– Diana E. H. Russell, researcher on sexual violence against women and girls

29% of child abuse offenders are relatives, 60% are acquaintances, and only 11% are strangers.
– Diana Russell, *The Secret Trauma*

For the vast majority of child victimizers in State prison, the victim was someone they knew before the crime. 1/3 had committed their crime against their own child, about ½ had a relationship with the victim as a friend, acquaintance, or relative other than an offspring, about one in seven reported the victim to have been a stranger to them.
–Bureau of Justice Statistics (BJS) Survey of State Prison Inmates, 1991

¾ of the violent victimizations of children took place in either the victim's home or the offender's home.
– Bureau of Justice Statistics (BJS) Survey of State Prison Inmates, 1991

Males are reported to be the abusers in 80-95%.
– Thoringer, D., et al., 1988

All but 3% of offenders who committed violent crimes against children were male.
– Bureau of Justice Statistics (BJS) Survey of State Prison Inmates, 1991

The typical offender is male, begins molesting by age 15, engages in a variety of deviant behavior, and molests an average of 117 youngsters, most of whom do not report the offence.
– Dr. Gene Abel

Offenders who had victimized a child were on average five years or older than the the violent offenders who had committed their crime against adults. Nearly 25% of child victimizers were age 40 or older, but about 10% of the inmates with adult victims fell in that range.
– Bureau of Justice Statistics (BJS) Survey of State Prison Inmates, 1991

71% of male offenders are under the age of 35.
– Dr. Ann Burgess, doctoral prepared, board-certified psychiatric clinical nurse specialist, and Dr. Nicholas Groth, American psychologist, in a study of imprisoned offenders

¾ of sexual predators are younger than 35. About 80% are of normal intelligence or above.
– Profiles from the FBI Academy and the National Center for Missing and Exploited Children

Many clinical settings currently are witnessing a dramatic increase in the number of adolescent offenders who have committed sexually aggressive acts against other children.
– Jon R. Conte, Past President, American Professional Society on the Abuse of Children

While nearly 70% of those serving time for violent crimes against children were white, whites accounted for 40% of those imprisoned for violent crimes against adults.

– Bureau of Justice Statistics (BJS) Survey of State Prison Inmates, 1991

Inmates who victimized children were less likely than other inmates to have prior criminal record; nearly 1/3 of child victimizers had never been arrested prior to the current offence, compared to less than 20% of those who victimized adults.

– Bureau of Justice Statistics (BJS) Survey of State Prison Inmates, 1991

Violent child victimizers were substantially more likely than those with adult victims to have been physically or sexually abused when they were children.

– Bureau of Justice Statistics (BJS) Survey of State Prison Inmates, 1991

50% of reported child molestations involve the use of physical force and child molesters produce as much visible physical injury as rapists – 39% of victims.

– Dr. Gene Abel

About 14% of child victimizers carried a weapon during the violent crime, compared to nearly ½ of those who victimized adults.

– Bureau of Justice Statistics (BJS) Survey of State Prison Inmates, 1991

About 10% of violent offenders with child victims received life or death sentences and the average prison term was 11years, somewhat shorter average sentences that received by those with adult victims.

– Bureau of Justice Statistics (BJS) Survey of State Prison Inmates, 1991

More than ½ of all convicted sex offenders are sent back to prison within a year. Within two years, 77.9% are back.

– California Department of Corrections

Recidivism rates range from 18-45%; the more violent the crime the more likely of repeating.

– Studies by the State of Washington

Three in ten child victimizers reported that they had committed their crimes against multiple victims; they were more likely than those who victimized adults to have had multiple victims.
– Bureau of Justice Statistics (BJS) Survey of State Prison Inmates, 1991

Like rape, child molestation is one of the most underreported crimes; only 1 – 10% are ever disclosed.
– FBI Law Enforcement Bulletin

The behavior is highly repetitive, to the point of compulsion, rather than resulting from a lack of judgment.
– Dr. Ann Burgess and Dr. Nicholas Groth, et al. in a study of imprisoned offenders.

Appendix

Treatment Program Brochures

Treatment Program for Sex Offender Clergymen
Dr. Leo R. Theriault

Model of Treatment

It is a modular program based on the Relapse Prevention Model. This model is a cognitive behavioral approach. It believes that sex offenders do not "just happen", but are the result of a chain of actions leading to the offense. Therefore the offense can be prevented by recognizing the chain of events and breaking it at any time before the relapse.

Objectives

Break through denial

Recognize the consequences of abuse on the victims

Confront offences with shepherd's responsibility towards Christ's flock especially with children

Recognition of one's chain of actions preceding and leading to offences

Establish a realistic relapse prevention plan

Recognize the difference between animal, human and Christian sexuality

Recognize how love and sexuality can be either fulfilling or destructive, and why

Duration of Treatment

It is a four week program consisting of one hundred (100) hours of intensive group therapy and many hours of homework

Schedule

MONDAY through FRIDAY

2.5 hours am therapy

2.5 hours pm therapy

Evening homework

SATURDAY

Day trip tours of Arizona

SUNDAY
Church attendance in the morning
Relaxing activities in afternoons

FOURTH WEEK
It is strongly recommended that the bishop, or a bishop appointed priest, attend this portion of treatment with the client. The bishop (or the appointed priest) would then be aware of the offender's problems and of his relapse prevention plan. This person would have the responsibility of a long-term follow-up and also of organizing and lending a support group for sex offender priests in the diocese. This priest must not be a recovering sex offender himself. This therapist does not believe in the blind leading the blind.

Anonymity
Anonymity will be respected except when the law dictates as in the case of convicted sex offenders.

Number of Clients
Group therapy has proven to me more efficient in the treatment of sex offence than individual therapy. The therapist will take no less than two and no more than five clients at one time, aiming at an ideal number of three or four.

Therapist
Dr. Leo R. Theriault
Psy.D. CPC Arizona.
Registered psychologist in New Brunswick, Canada since 1969.
Ford Foundation Fellow
Ordained priest in 1958

Where
In Wickenburg, Arizona, on a 2.5 acre parcel of desert land. The "cowboy town" of Wickenburg is located one hour North West of Phoenix. The population fluctuates from 6000 in the summer to about double in the winter season.
The clients will be restricted to this safe and beautiful environment unless escorted in group to the schedule of events

For more information please contact:
Dr. Leo Theriault
701 South Saguaro Drive
Wickenburg, AZ 85390
(520) 684-1177 fax (520) 684-1255

Just What The Doctor Ordered...

An

INTENSIVE

THERAPY

RETREAT

An effective and productive approach of therapy while in the serene and safe environment of Dr. Theriault's desert life setting.

"Just What the Doctor Ordered"

HOW

Does Therapy Work?

Therapy works by helping you objectively look at behaviors, feelings and thoughts in situations which you find problematic. It helps you to learn more effective ways of dealing with those situations.

Therapy is a collective effort. You and your therapist will identify your goals – what you want to have happen, and agree on how you'll know when you're making progress.

WHAT

Is Dr. Theriault's Approach

His approach is eclectic, but he puts emphasis on the Cognitive-Behavioral approach. He listens and understands, but he also explains and supports when appropriate.

He uses the Relapse Prevention Model in treating substance abuse and sexual abuse.

His Fundamental Beliefs in Therapy?

He believes that people of normal intelligence have within themselves all that is needed to solve their own problems. The have within the seeds of their own recovery.

No therapist can "fix problems" as a motor mechanic – but can supply the proper environment to permit the person to grow as a gardener would do. This growth can be a very long process, but Dr. Theriault favors short-term therapy of 6 to 10 hours, which has had excellent results in most cases.

For More Information or Reservations

Please Contact...

WHY

Intensive Therapy Retreat

This Intensive Therapy Retreat offers a twofold nurturing experience. He has found that longer sessions of uninterrupted time allow a continuum of focused energy for his clients, resulting in a quicker recovery process with greater satisfaction,. Many people prefer intensive therapy to weekly or bimonthly sessions for these exact reasons. Dr. Theriault offers this opportunity.

Upon request and reservation in advance, Dr. Theriault will reserve a day or two, on the weekend or during the week, for 3 to 5 hours of therapy per day. Dr. Theriault will be at the sole disposition of the **person**, the **couple** or the **family** involved.

WHERE

Wickenburg, AZ has become the home for Dr. and Mrs. Theriault. Nestled approximately 40 miles West of Phoenix, the terrain is rolling hills filled with saguaro, ocotillo and much desert wildlife. His parcel layout allows for private sessions in his separate office building down a path of peaceful desert with lazy lizards and blue skies.

If lodging is desired, "Chez Rina Bed & Breakfast" is owned and operated by his charming French Canadian wife, Rina. It is on the 2.6 acre spot with terrific vistas to enjoy the sunrise, sunset, & mountains. Quail, rabbits, the sounds of owls and coyotes at night and an occasional deer help provide to a true desert experience. The Theriault's and Wickenburg have a lot to offer.

Dr. Leo Theriault

701 South Saguaro Drive, PO Box 20370

Wickenburg, AZ 85358

WHO

Dr. Leo Theriault (pronounced Tay-Rio)

A French Canadian from New Brunswick, Canada, he is an Acadian cousin of the Cajuns of Louisiana. He moved to Wickenburg, Arizona bringing with him over 30 years of experience as a clinical psychologist.

He was the father figure in a group home for homeless teenagers for 10 years. He successfully completed a six year contract with Correctional Service Canada for the treatment of parolees. He provided three, 14 week group therapy programs for French sexual offenders in the New Brunswick prison system.

EAP Therapist contracted by New Brunswick Power, New Brunswick Telephone and Extra Mural Hospital in New Brunswick.

Psychotherapy with incestuous families; the offender, the spouse and the victim(s).

Counselor in long term residential substance abuse program in Phoenix prior to moving to Wickenburg.

He is very efficient in the treatment of teenagers, depression, marital problems and sexual disorders.

He is an excellent facilitator in group dynamics and an experienced lecturer.

(520) 684-1174

Fax (520) 683-1255

Credentials

PROFESSIONAL

Dr. Theriault is a registered psychologist of the College of Psychologists of New Brunswick in Canada since 1969.

He is an active member of the Canadian Psychological Association.

EDUCATION

Doctor of Psychology, 1985

Heed University, LA

Education Credential Evaluators, Inc.

Milwaukee, Wisconsin, 10 June 1997

"It is the judgment of Educational Credential Evaluators, Inc. that Leo R. Theriault has the equivalent of a Bachelor of Arts degree with a major in Catholic Theology in the United States; a Master of Arts Degree in Catholic Theology; and completion of an additional undergraduate major in Educational Psychology. This evaluation does not include any academic works completed in the United States."

F.F.F.: Ford Foundation Fellowship

Leadership Development Program 1972. During that year of fellowship, Dr. Theriault had the opportunity to visit reform schools, group homes and treatment centers through North America. Of particular interest is the private meeting with Dr. Bruno Bettelheim and spending three days at his school for autistic children.

Dr. Clarence Jeffrey, "Leo is a professional in the profession!" Jeffrey had been a university professor of Leo's and later a colleague.

Dr. Leo Theriault

701 South Saguaro Drive, PO Box 20370

Wickenburg, AZ 85358

Thought of a Prayer

When I get angry it makes me upset,
I then do something to later regret,
But this time I'm gonna write a poem to help me,
It's gonna be my prayer to ask Jesus to sit me free,
I have never been able to manage my anger in the right way,
My anger don't allow me to think about what I do or say,
My anger has caused me to teach only negative to my brother,
Which will only lead to him later hurting my caring mother,
Because that is all I have done to her over the past couple years,
I have always been in jail never at home to share her cheers,
I have respected my friends more than my dad,
Been told this by him and only feld mad,
I have hurt my little sister, so many time made her sad,
Because I wood do crimes with my friends to feel Big and bad,
I have led my family through all this pain,
Because of the drug I wood put into my vein,
In the past I have thought of what I have done,
It made me come to the conclusion to pick up a gun,
I placed the cold steal into my mouth,
Then thought do I want to go North or South,
As I thought in my head is this for real,
I decided their's other ways for this wound to heel,
That's when I realized I have thought while I was mad,
But with this thought came happiness that made me sad,
Because I finally realized I'm making my life a crime,
And considering the people in it not worth as much as a dime,
Writing this poem has made me decide,
To get on that bus that gives god's ride,
Because I don't want to hurt my family again,
And I don't want to live my life in prison,
So I ask you dear Jesus please help my out,
And forgive me of my sins and send me about.